W9-CCQ-273

STARTING
Your Own Business: Become an Entrepreneur!

by Adam Toren and Matthew Toren

Entrepreneurs and Brothers

WILEY

STARTING YOUR OWN BUSINESS: BECOME AN ENTREPRENEUR!

Published by:
John Wiley & Sons, Inc.,
111 River Street,
Hoboken, NJ 07030-5774,

www.wiley.com

Copyright © 2017 by John Wiley & Sons, Inc., Hoboken, New Jersey

Published simultaneously in Canada

No part of this publication may be reproduced, stored in a retrieval system or transmitted in any form or by any means, electronic, mechanical, photocopying, recording, scanning or otherwise, except as permitted under Sections 107 or 108 of the 1976 United States Copyright Act, without the prior written permission of the Publisher. Requests to the Publisher for permission should be addressed to the Permissions Department, John Wiley & Sons, Inc., 111 River Street, Hoboken, NJ 07030, (201) 748-6011, fax (201) 748-6008, or online at http://www.wiley.com/go/permissions.

Trademarks: Wiley, For Dummies, the Dummies Man logo, Dummies.com, Making Everything Easier, and related trade dress are trademarks or registered trademarks of John Wiley & Sons, Inc. and may not be used without written permission. All other trademarks are the property of their respective owners. John Wiley & Sons, Inc. is not associated with any product or vendor mentioned in this book.

LIMIT OF LIABILITY/DISCLAIMER OF WARRANTY: THE PUBLISHER AND THE AUTHOR MAKE NO REPRESENTATIONS OR WARRANTIES WITH RESPECT TO THE ACCURACY OR COMPLETENESS OF THE CONTENTS OF THIS WORK AND SPECIFICALLY DISCLAIM ALL WARRANTIES, INCLUDING WITHOUT LIMITATION WARRANTIES OF FITNESS FOR A PARTICULAR PURPOSE. NO WARRANTY MAY BE CREATED OR EXTENDED BY SALES OR PROMOTIONAL MATERIALS. THE ADVICE AND STRATEGIES CONTAINED HEREIN MAY NOT BE SUITABLE FOR EVERY SITUATION. THIS WORK IS SOLD WITH THE UNDERSTANDING THAT THE PUBLISHER IS NOT ENGAGED IN RENDERING LEGAL, ACCOUNTING, OR OTHER PROFESSIONAL SERVICES. IF PROFESSIONAL ASSISTANCE IS REQUIRED, THE SERVICES OF A COMPETENT PROFESSIONAL PERSON SHOULD BE SOUGHT. NEITHER THE PUBLISHER NOR THE AUTHOR SHALL BE LIABLE FOR DAMAGES ARISING HEREFROM. THE FACT THAT AN ORGANIZATION OR WEBSITE IS REFERRED TO IN THIS WORK AS A CITATION AND/OR A POTENTIAL SOURCE OF FURTHER INFORMATION DOES NOT MEAN THAT THE AUTHOR OR THE PUBLISHER ENDORSES THE INFORMATION THE ORGANIZATION OR WEBSITE MAY PROVIDE OR RECOMMENDATIONS IT MAY MAKE. FURTHER, READERS SHOULD BE AWARE THAT INTERNET WEBSITES LISTED IN THIS WORK MAY HAVE CHANGED OR DISAPPEARED BETWEEN WHEN THIS WORK WAS WRITTEN AND WHEN IT IS READ.

For general information on our other products and services, please contact our Customer Care Department within the U.S. at 877-762-2974, outside the U.S. at 317-572-3993, or fax 317-572-4002. For technical support, please visit https://hub.wiley.com/community/support/dummies.

Wiley publishes in a variety of print and electronic formats and by print-on-demand. Some material included with standard print versions of this book may not be included in e-books or in print-on-demand. If this book refers to media such as a CD or DVD that is not included in the version you purchased, you may download this material at http://booksupport.wiley.com. For more information about Wiley products, visit www.wiley.com.

Library of Congress Control Number: 2017934299

ISBN 978-1-119-27164-2 (pbk); ISBN 978-1-119-27178-9 (ePub); 978-1-119-27181-9 (ePDF)

Manufactured in the United States of America

10 9 8 7 6 5 4 3 2 1

CONTENTS

PROJECT 2: FIND YOUR BIG IDEA 19

PROJECT 3: MAKE A PLAN 33

PROJECT 4: KNOW WHAT TO DO WITH YOUR SHINY NEW BUSINESS PLAN 53

PROJECT 5: BUDGET FOR SUCCESS 60

PROJECT 6: PLAN YOUR MARKETING   74

PROJECT 7: SET UP SHOP   84

PROJECT 8: SERVICE 101   106

WORDS OF ENCOURAGEMENT   116

GLOSSARY   118

INTRODUCTION

SO, YOU WANT TO START YOUR OWN BUSINESS. That's awesome!

Starting and running your own business can be one of the most fun and rewarding experiences there is.

Just look around your town and on the Internet at all the businesses that exist today. You'll find retail stores, restaurants, software companies, mobile phone companies, car repair shops, delivery services, hair salons, and thousands more businesses.

Now think about this: Every one of those businesses was originally started by a person who had an idea and decided to make it into a business. Some did it on their own, and others had teams of people right from the start. Either way, they weren't very different from you — except they probably weren't thinking of starting a business when they were your age. That means you have a huge head start in the world of entrepreneurship. Good for you!

Is starting a business hard? Sometimes. Does it take a lot of time? It can. Is it risky? Often it is, yes. But is it all worth it? Definitely! There is something very special about starting and growing a business that makes most entrepreneurs feel like it's more than worth all the hard work, time, and risk.

That "something special" can be hard to explain. It's the excitement of building something of your own; it's the thrill of selling your first product or service; it's the feeling that you're doing something you love and helping people at the same time. It is why millions of people start businesses every year, and it's why many people keep starting one business after another. These people sometimes have several businesses at once. If these folks are willing to increase the work, time, and risk they put into one business many times over, you know there must be a strong appeal to business ownership.

Now it's time for you to experience the rewards of starting your own business. Dig in, and start your journey right away. We know you'll love it!

ABOUT THIS BOOK

By completing the projects in this book, you'll be able to take all the steps necessary to be an entrepreneur, at any age.

Whether you just want some extra money to buy something new or you're interested in building a business that you'll run for many years, you can find what you need in this book.

We cover all the topics you'd find in a book for adults, but we break them down and explain them just for kids. Topics include

- » How to come up with a great business idea

- » How to plan for your business to be successful

- » How to handle the money in your business

- » How to get the word out so that everyone knows about your new business

- » How to launch and run your business

- » How to take care of your customers

After you complete the projects outlined in this book, you'll come away with a real business that you can grow to whatever level you want.

Complete the worksheets, quizzes, and forms in this book and keep the book handy so that you can refer to those items. Having this information as a reference is great because a few months from now, you won't remember everything you were thinking of today.

In addition to the fill-in-the-blank pages in the book, we also recommend you keep a notebook handy while going through each project. Use the notebook to write down any points you think will be important when you start putting the tasks in the book into practice. In fact, most successful business owners keep a notebook with them at all times because they never know when a great idea will strike!

ABOUT YOU

If you're interested in starting a business, we assume that you have some spare time. You should have access to a computer (with a parent's permission). If you don't have a computer available at home, check out your local library. They usually have computers you can use for free.

Lastly, we hope you know how important school is and that you won't let starting a business distract you from your studies. The projects in this book are meant to be completed outside your school and any activities you participate in.

ABOUT THE ICONS

As you read through the projects in this book, you'll see some icons. The icons point out different things:

Remember icon alerts you to points that are especially important for you to remember.

When you see the Tip icon, we're giving you information that will help you throughout your entrepreneurial journey.

PROJECT 1 GET DOWN TO BASICS

BEFORE JUMPING INTO STARTING A BUSINESS, IT'S IMPORTANT TO KNOW EXACTLY WHAT ENTREPRENEURSHIP IS AND IF IT'S SOMETHING THAT REALLY APPEALS TO YOU.

What are the advantages and disadvantages of having your own business versus working as an employee? What will you probably love about being an entrepreneur, and what challenges are you likely to face?

This project helps you work through the answers to those questions and much more.

ENTREPRENEURSHIP EXPLAINED

What is entrepreneurship? *Entrepreneurship* is simply the act of being an entrepreneur. It's what an entrepreneur — someone who owns his or her own business — does. Anyone who owns a business can be called an entrepreneur. But true entrepreneurs start businesses on their own, or with partners, and work hard to grow those businesses — and they usually love doing it!

Entrepreneurs aren't just business owners. They thrive on starting and building businesses, and many start several businesses over a lifetime. Some of their businesses are successes, and some are not. But the mark of a true entrepreneur is that he never stops trying. True entrepreneurs are excited about their successful companies, and when something they build fails, they see it as a chance to learn and do better next time.

Another part of what it means to be an entrepreneur is dealing with people who don't share in your vision. Chances are high that not everyone will be as supportive as possible during your journey through entrepreneurship. You may experience resistance or criticism from parents, friends, or others you meet. But remember, if you want to be an entrepreneur, you are doing it for you — not because of what someone else thinks. You can't let anyone or anything stand in your way.

DISCOVERING WHAT'S AWESOME ABOUT BEING AN ENTREPRENEUR

Becoming an entrepreneur can be very rewarding. In fact, most people who have started their own businesses would not want to do anything else. Once you've experienced entrepreneurship, it might just be the only thing you ever want to do for work.

The following sections look at some of the great things about being an entrepreneur, and some of the challenges you're likely to face along the way.

FREEDOM

If you asked entrepreneurs what they like most about having their own business, many would put freedom at the top of their list. What does *freedom* mean when it comes to entrepreneurship? You may have heard people refer to owning a business as "being your own boss." What they mean by this is that you, as the one who started and owns your company, are the one in charge. You don't have a boss to answer to, as you would if you had a job working for someone else.

Freedom can also mean being able to work at something you enjoy doing. Many people with jobs complain about their work a lot. An entrepreneur should be working only on a business she enjoys, and that can make a big difference in your happiness!

Of course, enjoying your work doesn't mean you don't have responsibilities. As we talk about later in this project, it isn't about being able to do whatever you want, whenever you want. To be a good business owner, you have to take great care of your customers and anyone who works for you, and you have duties that need to get done daily.

However, the kind of freedom that comes with owning a business versus having a job is what allows you to work the hours you prefer, work where you want, and hopefully do what you love as your source of income. An entrepreneur doesn't have to ask anyone to take a long lunch break or come in late.

What do you think will be the best part about owning your own business?

_____

_____

_____

_____

TIME

There's no question that starting a business does take a lot of time and hard work. In fact, it might take up most of your spare time — at least for a while. However, one great advantage of building your own business is that you can eventually have friends and family help with much of the work, allowing you to spend more time doing the things you love.

Many successful entrepreneurs are able to spend plenty of time with their families, travel all over the world, and take time out to enjoy activities that are meaningful to them. Whether you like boating, playing sports, or just hanging out by the pool, finding success in entrepreneurship can lead to more time to spend the way you want to spend it.

If you could decide what to do with your time, after school and homework, what are two to three things you'd enjoy spending time on?

_____

_____

_____

_____

MONEY

One reason people find entrepreneurship worthwhile is that it can be very rewarding financially. While it isn't common, some entrepreneurs, like Mark Zuckerberg (who started Facebook) and Bill Gates (the founder of Microsoft), have even become billionaires through entrepreneurship! Of course, building a company that can change the world isn't easy, but it's still true that a big advantage of starting your own business is that you can make good money doing it.

Some entrepreneurs build companies that do very well selling the product or service they make. This can create a great income for the business owner. Many live very well off the money their businesses earn, and that business becomes their livelihood for the rest of their lives. Other entrepreneurs build their business up and then sell the business, often to a larger company. The sale of a business can bring in a large sum of money and allow the entrepreneur who started the business to live comfortably for a long time.

Because most entrepreneurs love starting and building businesses, they often use the money from the sale of one business to start another business. People who start one business after another several times are sometimes called *serial entrepreneurs*. They enjoy the money from the businesses they start, but their main drive is the thrill of starting a business, as well as other advantages, like time and freedom.

If your business does well, what will you use your money for? List two to three things you'd like to buy or do with the extra money from your business:

_____

_____

_____

_____

UNDERSTANDING WHY ENTREPRENEURSHIP ISN'T ALWAYS AWESOME

At this point, being an entrepreneur sounds pretty good, right? Well, it is! Having your own business has many advantages, which is why so many people become entrepreneurs every year. As with anything, though, entrepreneurship isn't always easy. There are some challenges that every entrepreneur faces, and it's important that you know what those are.

MONEY

It's true that people get rich starting and owning businesses. It's also true that some people lose a lot of money trying to build a business that just doesn't end up working. When starting a business, an entrepreneur almost always has to spend some money to get it going. And once the business is up and running, there are expenses that need to be paid out to keep it going.

With proper planning, a smart business owner can avoid some of the risk that comes with opening a business. However, no one can see the future and plan for everything that could possibly happen. There is always some risk in starting a business, and that risk can sometimes lead to losing money.

Worldwide, entrepreneurs start about 50 million businesses each year, even after knowing the risk of losing money. So, for many, the potential of making a lot of money outweighs the chance they might lose money. It depends a lot on an entrepreneur's willingness to take a chance and her confidence in her business.

How would you feel if you lost money in business? Would you try again or call it quits? Why?

_____

_____

_____

_____

TIME

Time is a precious thing. We each have a limited amount of time in our days, and it's important to make the best of it. For most entrepreneurs, the extra time spent building their business is worth the reward when the business is successful.

For others, the amount of time it takes to start and run their business is much more than they bargained for. When unexpected challenges come up — or even when the business is more successful than they planned — many entrepreneurs are surprised how much of their time is taken up by their business.

It is important to balance the things you like and need to do (like spending time with friends and family and focusing on school) with the time it takes to tend to your growing business. Your business may be very important to you, and that's great, but if it's all you focus on, you might get tired of it pretty fast.

How much time each week are you willing to work on your new business? What will you do if more time is needed?

_____

_____

_____

_____

FREEDOM

Wait. How can "freedom" be listed under "What's not so awesome"? We agree that freedom is pretty awesome! But, believe it or not, not everyone does well when they are given the freedom to do what they want. Running your own business requires your time and attention. And because there isn't anyone telling you what to do and when to do it, being a business owner requires discipline.

Successful entrepreneurs are self-motivated and have the focus it takes to do what needs to be done without having anyone check up on them. But for many, it can be a challenge to focus on what needs to be done, while having the freedom to do whatever you want.

Also, because owning a business can be time consuming, entrepreneurs often find that even though they _can_ do what they want, the success of their business depends on them putting off the things that total freedom allows.

How do you feel when you have homework to do but really want to play video games or be on your phone or tablet? How do you focus on the task that's most important?

_____

_____

_____

_____

LOOKING AT COMMON TRAITS OF SUCCESSFUL BUSINESS OWNERS

Not all successful business owners are the same. Entrepreneurs come from just about every possible background. Some grew up with money, while some were very poor. Some had parents who were entrepreneurs, and others were raised in families where everyone worked at traditional jobs. So, no matter who you are, you can become a successful entrepreneur.

Even with all their various backgrounds, those who make it big as business owners share some common traits. Learning about and growing in these areas will make it easier for you to find success in business ownership.

BACKGROUND

No matter what your family has done for work in the past and whether you come from a wealthy or poor background, you _can_ be successful. However, those with a history of wanting to learn and seeing the value of hard work have a huge advantage. One sign that you have what it takes to be a success is that you're reading this book!

Making it your lifelong goal to keep learning will help you in whatever you do. It is what separates people who are mega-successful from those who struggle to get by. It's true that the more you know, the easier it is to accomplish your goals.

Being willing to work hard to get what you want is the second part of this "formula for success." You can have all the knowledge possible about a subject, but if you don't use that knowledge to work toward your goals, it won't do you any good. Whatever your background has been like so far, make your willingness to work hard part of your background from now on.

PERSONALITY

If you meet 100 entrepreneurs, you'll find 100 individual personalities. Because entrepreneurs come from a wide range of backgrounds, they vary a lot in their personalities as well. Successful entrepreneurs, however, share certain personality traits.

First, most successful business owners are good with people. They may or may not be super outgoing, but when they interact with people, they're able to get along well and generally well liked. Think about it. As a business owner, you will interact with customers, vendors (people you buy from), and at some point, employees. If you are good with people — meaning you get along well and are friendly and easy to work with — it will help you in all your relationships.

Another personality trait common to successful entrepreneurs is that they are positive people. Being positive means seeing the good in people and in things that happen in everyday life. For example, you may hear a lot of people complain about Mondays, but an entrepreneur isn't likely to hate Mondays. Instead, they see every new week as a chance to learn more, accomplish more, and take another step toward success. And when an entrepreneur experiences failure of any kind, they certainly don't like it, but after getting over the disappointment, they see failures as learning experiences that will make them better in the long run.

ATTITUDE

A positive attitude is something that is very important for success in anything you do. In school, sports, and friendships, whether you decide to be a business owner or work for someone else, having a great attitude will help you reach your goals — and enjoy the journey!

So, what does it mean to have a positive attitude? It is having *a can-do approach* to life. A can-do approach means that you see that anything is possible, and you don't let anyone or anything get in the way of a goal that is important to you. Instead of letting bad situations get you down, you find the silver lining.

When you have a great attitude, you don't complain, and you don't put things off. You do what needs to be done with a smile on your face because you realize that every task is a chance to learn and grow — or a chance to go do something more fun if you get it done quickly!

To find out whether entrepreneurship a good fit for you, take the quiz!

Is entrepreneurship a good fit for you?

For each statement below, circle either True or False. Then count up the number of statements you marked as True and compare it with the section at the bottom of the quiz.

1. **Among my group of friends, I am a leader.**
   True   False

2. **I like to figure out how things work.**
   True   False

3. **When I don't succeed at something the first time, I keep trying until I'm good at it.**
   True   False

4. **I enjoy competing in sports and/or games.**
   True   False

5. **I get along well with other kids, teachers, and parents.**
   True   False

6. **Someone in my family owns his or her own business.**
   True   False

7. **I don't mind trying something new, even though it might not work.**
   True   False

8. **I do my homework and household chores without a lot of reminders from my parents.**
   True   False

9. **I have a great imagination.**
   True   False

10. **When something is important to me, I refuse to give up.**
    True   False

How many did you mark as true?

8–10 You are made for entrepreneurship! You have what it takes to be an entrepreneur, and you will love starting and owning your own business. Best of all, you have a great chance of being successful if you stay on course and refuse to give up, even when things aren't so easy.

5–7 You have what it takes to be a successful entrepreneur! The most important thing for you to remember is to keep trying, even if you don't feel like it or if things are hard. Keep learning about entrepreneurship and give it all you've got, and you'll do well.

0–4 It might seem like having your own business is a lot of work or that it is even a little scary. But don't let that keep you from learning more about entrepreneurship and giving it a try. You may just surprise yourself. Many successful entrepreneurs started out not thinking they would ever own their own businesses and then ended up doing really well.

COMPARING A JOB TO OWNING A BUSINESS

Even though this book is about entrepreneurship, and we encourage people to own their own businesses, we know that owning a business isn't for everyone. Each path has advantages and disadvantages (see Table 1-1).

TABLE 1-1   ENTREPRENEUR OR EMPLOYEE?

Entrepreneur	Employee
Works the hours she sets	Works hours she's told to work
May not get a steady paycheck	Generally gets a regular paycheck
Responsible for whole business	Responsible for only her job
Risks her own money	No investment of personal money
Can hire helpers (employees) to complete tasks she doesn't want to do	Must do the work assigned

The following sections take a deeper look at a couple areas that many people focus on when deciding whether they want to work for someone or own a business.

STABILITY

When it comes to making a living, *stability* means that there is a good chance you'll be in the same job tomorrow as you are today. It means not having to worry that your job (or company) will go away at any time.

When people have jobs, they often feel like they have stability. They might work for a big company that is doing well, or they know that their boss is happy with their work, so they aren't likely to get fired. However, even the biggest companies reduce the number of workers they need from time to time and *lay off people*. That means a worker is told his services are no longer needed at the company. It isn't the same as being fired, but the result is the same: The worker loses his job.

As a business owner, you have more control over the stability of your work. If you are smart and you look for trends in your area of work, plan, and stay focused, you can greatly reduce the risk of your company closing. The chance is still there, though, so starting a business comes with a risk, just as there is with having a job.

What we like about business ownership is that even if your business closes, you can start a new business using much of what you learned with your last business. If you are fired or laid off from your job, it might take a long time to find another job, and your future is in the hands of people who may or may not hire you.

SECURITY

When we talk about *security* in the work you do, it has to do with stability, but it's more focused on the money you make. When you have a job, you get a paycheck from your employer, and you usually know exactly how much each paycheck is going to be and what date you'll receive it. People often feel secure in this situation because they're able to plan and budget their money. They think they know what their future holds, which gives them a sense of security.

But remember what we said about stability? The same thing is true of security: You can't always know for sure that you'll have a job tomorrow, and if your job goes away, so do your paychecks.

Entrepreneurship can be a lot scarier than a job, especially when you're an adult and have a family to support. Until your business has been around for a while and is stable, money might not come in a steady stream — or at all! It's that risk of not doing well that actually drives many entrepreneurs to succeed. True entreprenuers believe that the future is in their hands, and that they make their own security by working hard and being focused on their goals.

Of course, as a kid, you don't have to worry about supporting a family or having a job, which makes starting a business even more fun! It also means you have plenty of time to try out different ideas to find the one that works best.

List three reasons why you would like to become an entrepreneur.

_____

_____

_____

_____

PROJECT **2** *FIND YOUR BIG IDEA*

WE HOPE YOU'RE EXCITED TO GET STARTED CREATING YOUR OWN BUSINESS! Of course, before you can have a business, you must have an idea for a business. Every business in the world has started the same way: Someone had a great idea.

By completing this project, you will come up with lots of ideas and then figure out which idea is the best one for you. You'll also learn how to look at each idea and understand the pros and cons of your idea. From there, you'll know whether each idea will work as a business.

IDEAS FOR CREATING IDEAS

There are lots of ways to generate business ideas. You can surf the Internet for ideas, survey friends and family about what they would do, or daydream and hope something comes to you.

We're going to show you a way to come up with your own ideas and use your creativity to create a list of ideas, using just your brain and a piece of paper.

PREPARE FOR YOUR IDEA SESSION

Before beginning this project, it's important to set up your surroundings so that you can focus. Here's what to do:

1 Find a quiet place to work.

It could be your room, the library, or the kitchen table — as long as you won't be disturbed there.

2 Grab your notebook and open it to a clean, blank page.

3 Have two or three pens or pencils ready to go.

If you run out of ink or break the lead, you don't want to have to stop.

4 If it's allowed where you're going to be working, have a glass of cold water available so that you can quench your thirst without getting up.

WRITE UNTIL YOUR HAND HURTS

Are you ready to go? Good. This process is simple, but it's also really powerful. You're about to create a long list of ideas. You might just be surprised by how many ideas are hiding in your brain. This method of *brainstorming* (a way to come up with ideas and solve problems) is used by entrepreneurs and managers of small companies, as well as the largest organizations around. Learning how to brainstorm will help you in any field you decide to pursue.

You'll begin by listing business ideas in your notebook. You won't stop until you have at least ten, but don't stop at ten, if you can list more. List as many as you can think of. Here are some rules:

» Don't think about whether an idea is a good idea or not.

» List every idea you think of, even if it seems impossible or a little crazy.

» Don't try to figure out how you would make the idea work.

» Don't worry about what others might think of your idea.

» Have fun and use your imagination.

Business Ideas

Cupcake stand

Car washing service

Unicorn Farm

Handmade bracelets

Dog walking service

Sell candy door to door

Become a magician

Invent time machine

Garage organizing service

Dog washing service

Sell homemade candles

Tutoring service

The important point to remember is that this is just a list of ideas. You'll worry about deciding which ideas are good ones later.

So, get your pen or pencil ready, take a drink of water, and get writing!

How many ideas did you write in your notebook? If you had to write one more, what would you add?

_____

_____

_____

_____

LOOK AT YOUR WORLD WITH DIFFERENT EYES

After you have your list of ten or more ideas, you aren't done thinking of ideas forever. You can add to your list any time an idea pops into your head. For example, you might see a product and suddenly think of a way to make it better or easier to use. You could even wake up after dreaming of a great idea and then add that to your list. After making your list, you may begin to see the world differently — through the eyes of an entrepreneur.

To think of the best business ideas, it's important to know why businesses exist. In short, they exist to solve problems. A cupcake business solves the problem of people being hungry or wanting a treat. Clothing stores solve the need for clothes, and a wide variety of websites and *brick-and-mortar businesses* (those that are in a building, not just online) solve problems for people needing entertainment, information, or any number of products and services.

An entrepreneur sees opportunities everywhere. When they hear someone complaining about a problem, entrepreneurs think of possible ways to solve the problem and how they could make their solution into a business.

For example, say that your brother is complaining that he has to wash the family dog. It's messy, frustrating, and a lot of work. He says he wishes there was a better way. You recognize that if he is complaining about this, there's a good chance many other people have the same complaints. You may start thinking about what it would take to start a dog washing service. Or maybe you have a fantastic idea for an automatic dog washing machine! You put Scruffy into the machine, flip a switch, and he's scrubbed and dried in five minutes. Awesome!

When you're at school, watching TV at home, or in the car with Mom and Dad, look around and begin thinking of the problems you see and how they could be solved with a new business idea. This is how pretty much every item in your home was invented, from forks and spoons to shoes and computers. And it's how every other business was started, too: Someone saw a problem and came up with a solution.

As you continue to practice the skill of seeing the world through the eyes of an entrepreneur and thinking of creative solutions, you'll find that you have more ideas all the time. Be sure to write all these ideas in your notebook. You won't try to build them all, but who knows — you might just become a serial entrepreneur.

What is a chore or type of work that is done in the kitchen that you could make easier with a brand new invention? What would your invention do, and how would it be helpful?

_____

_____

_____

_____

Look around at the appliances and tools that are in your kitchen. What tool or appliance would be better with some

sort of change to how it works? Would your change make it faster, easier, cheaper, or have some other advantage?

_____

_____

_____

_____

What is something your teacher must do every day that would be easier with some kind of new product or service? What could you invent to help teachers in their job?

_____

_____

_____

_____

Think of something that doesn't currently exist, but that the kids at your school would love to play with or use if it did. If you had a magic wand and could create it, how would this new thing change things at your school or for the world?

_____

_____

_____

_____

LOOK INTO THE FUTURE

While you're looking for problems and solutions, consider what the future will look like. Now, we don't expect you to be a psychic. However, what you can do is guess what kinds of changes the world is likely to see in the coming years.

For example, most people agree that at some point in the next ten years, most or all cars on the road will be self-driving. In fact, many believe that once all cars are self-driving, it will no longer be legal for people to drive their own cars.

How might this change things for people? Well, for one thing, people will be looking for something to do while taking long trips in their cars. Also, because there will be fewer accidents, tow truck drivers might not be needed as much as they are today. What businesses could be created to solve these problems?

No one knows for sure what the future holds, but beginning to think about what is likely to change can help you think of many more ideas. So, start looking into the future.

List three things you think will be different about the world in ten years.

_____

_____

_____

_____

THINK ABOUT WHAT YOU LOVE TO DO

Another way to come up with great business ideas is to think about what you love to do. Many entrepreneurs have built amazing businesses out of something they loved doing.

Do you like the game Minecraft? If so, chances are good that you watch Minecraft videos on YouTube. What you might not know is that many of the people who create those videos make quite a bit of money doing it. They get a small amount of money for the advertising placed on each video, which adds up, especially when they have thousands or millions of views. The people who make those videos have created a small business doing something they love.

What do you love to do? Whether you're into baseball, doll collecting, video games, or something else, you may be able to create a business from your favorite things.

So, when you're thinking of businesses to add to your growing list of ideas, consider the things you love to do. If you can create a business from something you really enjoy, it won't ever feel like work. You'll love what you're doing and probably will do very well at it.

What is your favorite thing to do? How could that be made into a business?

_____

_____

_____

_____

PICK THE BEST IDEA

You probably have a pretty long list of business ideas. Some may seem silly, but that's okay! It's great to use your imagination and let the ideas flow without overthinking them. That's how some amazing companies have been created.

Once your list is full of ideas, you're ready to figure out which ideas are the best options for you. Some of your ideas may be fantastic, but they may not be right for you right now. For example, if you want to build a better rocket to get astronauts into space, you'll probably need to wait until you've had plenty of schooling about how rockets work.

Other ideas may take years to build. That's fine, but with your first business, it's best to start with something you can get going on quickly. Once you have started one business, you'll have learned a lot about what to do, what not to do, and what you like best about entrepreneurship.

There are other considerations, too. In the following sections, you'll learn to evaluate your ideas to narrow down your results and pick the few that are the very best.

Before you begin evaluating your ideas, narrow down your list. If you have ideas that aren't possible right now (like helping NASA build a better rocket or mowing lawns in the middle of winter in Montana), put those aside for now. Next, eliminate any ideas that seem too dangerous or just don't sound fun to you, as well as any ideas that are likely impossible, like a unicorn farm.

Keep taking ideas off the list until you are left with three to five of your favorites. Then use the instructions in the rest of this project to narrow your list even further.

LOOK AT RISKS AND REWARDS

Did you know that everything you do has risks and rewards? A *risk* is basically anything that can go wrong. A *reward* is any positive outcome. Here are a couple of examples.

Taking a shower

Risks:

» You could slip and fall.

» You might get soap in your eyes.

» The water may be too hot or too cold.

Rewards:

» You'll feel clean after your shower.

» Your mom won't need to bug you to take a shower (for a while at least).

» Kids at school will not avoid you because you smell bad!

Playing video games:

Risks:

» You could get focused on your game and not hear your dad call you for dinner.

» Your device might overheat.

» The game may freeze up, causing you to lose your level and start over (ugh!).

Rewards:

» You'll have fun.

» You might improve your hand-eye coordination.

» If it's a multi-player game, you can interact with your friends.

As you can see, risks can vary from something that wouldn't be so bad to something that could be really serious. And the same goes for rewards. Some are minor, and others are quite important.

 The key is to figure out whether the possible risks are worth the potential rewards.

What are two to three risks for your favorite business idea on your list?

_____

_____

_____

_____

What are two to three rewards for your favorite business idea on your list?

_____

_____

_____

_____

CONSIDER HIDDEN RISKS

While reviewing your list of ideas, some risks will be obvious, and others will be more hidden. For example, say that one of your ideas is a cupcake stand. An obvious risk may be that keeping the cupcakes from getting stale could be a challenge. A hidden risk (or something you may not think of right away) is that bees could start hanging around your cupcake stand, scaring off your customers.

Entrepreneurship is full of surprises. Chances are good that you won't ever think of every possible risk that could come up, and that's okay. Each time something happens that you didn't expect, it's a chance for you to learn. Then, when you build another business or want to expand your business, you'll have more knowledge about what to expect.

HIDDEN REWARDS

The good news is that just as there are hidden risks, there are often hidden rewards. You'll have a list of rewards to help you decide to move forward with an idea, but other rewards or opportunities will surely come up while you're running your business.

Think about the cupcake stand, for example. An obvious reward is that you can make some money. A hidden reward may be that an executive from a grocery store chain tries your cupcakes, proclaims them to be the best she has ever tasted, and wants to sell your cupcakes at all her stores!

MAKE A LIST OF PROS AND CONS

Pros and cons are like risks and rewards, but a little different. A risk or reward is something that *might* happen. You might have bees around your cupcake stand, and you might make some good money selling cupcakes.

A *pro* or *con* is something that is a natural part of the business. A pro of having a cupcake stand is that you get to be outside. There's no question about that. A con is that you'll have to stay in one place for a while, waiting for or serving customers.

It's important to list the pros and cons for your business ideas, because while risks and rewards can tell you whether the business is a safe bet, pros and cons will help you decide whether the business is right for *you*. If you don't like staying in one place waiting for and serving customers, the cupcake stand may not be the best idea for you, even though it could be a good business for someone who doesn't mind standing around.

What are two to three pros for your favorite business idea on your list?

_____

_____

_____

_____

What are two to three cons for your favorite business idea on your list?

_____

_____

_____

_____

LISTEN TO YOUR GUT

When deciding on a business to start, most entrepreneurs don't rely only on risks, rewards, pros, and cons. They listen to their gut. What does that mean? It's not easy to explain, but *listening to your gut* is a feeling you have inside when you think about an idea.

ARE YOU EXCITED?

When you think about your idea, do you get excited? When you picture yourself doing what you'll do in your business, does it make you feel happy? Entrepreneurs do best when they build a business that excites them and makes them feel good when they think about it.

Be aware of the risks and the cons, but if you're excited about the possibility of pursuing your idea despite those, then your idea could still be a great fit for you.

WHAT DOES THAT LITTLE VOICE SAY?

What if you're having trouble deciding whether an idea is the right one? What if you have two great ideas and can't decide between them? This is where listening to that little voice in your head comes in. The little voice we're talking about may not actually be a voice telling you what to do. It's more of a feeling, similar to a gut feeling. But to many, it feels like a voice nudging them in one direction or another.

Take some time in a quiet place to think about each idea. If you pay close attention to how you feel while thinking of your ideas, you'll be able to tell which one is right for you.

What are your top two business ideas?

_____

_____

_____

_____

PICK A WINNER

After you evaluate your long list of ideas to see which ones are the best for you, it's finally time to pick a winner. You may already know which idea is perfect for you, but if not, don't worry. Here are some additional guidelines to help you:

Your winning idea should be. . .

» Something you can start right away

» An idea that won't take more money to start than you have

» Something you have time for (can be done after school and on weekends, for example)

» Something that's fun

You might also want to consider picking an idea that your parents can help you with. This is your idea and your business, but having support is always good. If you have an idea you like and it's also an idea your parents know something about, that's great!

What is your winning business idea?

_____

In a few sentences, explain your idea:

_____
_____
_____
_____
_____

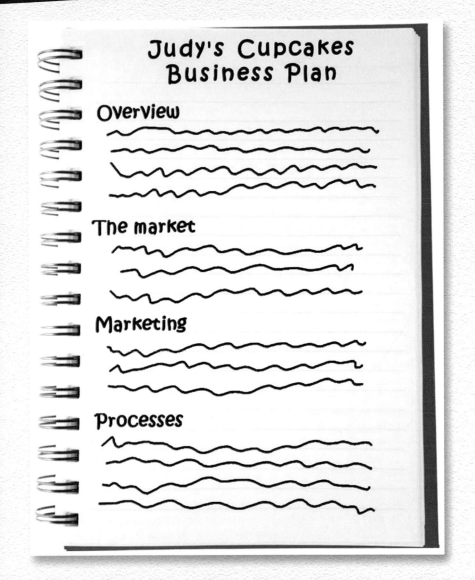

Judy's Cupcakes Business Plan

Overview

The market

Marketing

Processes

AFTER YOU'VE CHOSEN AN IDEA FOR YOUR BUSINESS, YOU'RE READY TO START PLANNING FOR SUCCESS. For large businesses that are looking for investors, a formal business plan is necessary. But for small businesses just getting started, a much shorter, simpler plan is best. In this project, you'll create a simple plan for your new business, and you'll learn how to use your plan to guide you as your business grows.

THE PURPOSE OF A BUSINESS PLAN

Your *business plan* is an outline of your business that explains what your business is all about and how it operates. It is the guiding document for your business. In other words, it shows you the path forward at every stage of your business. With a great business plan in place, you won't have to wonder what to do next, and you will be able to measure your progress against your plan to make sure that you're on track at all times.

Large companies create very long, detailed business plans that are filled with lots of statistics, graphs, and explanations of every aspect of the business, as well as detailed forecasts for growth. For those businesses, it's important to be that detailed, but for most small businesses, so much detail just isn't necessary. Your plan won't be used to get investors or acquire a bank loan, so even though a plan is still a valuable tool for your business, it can be pretty simple if you want it to be.

Why do you think planning is important before you start your business?

_____

_____

_____

_____

WHO WILL SEE IT

Some business plans are meant to be seen by investors, bankers, or consultants. The business plan you create in this project is mostly for your own use. It isn't something you'll share with your customers or anyone else who is not part of your business.

You may decide to show parts of it to partners or key employees, if you ever have them, and if you have advisers (your parents, for example), you'll want to share it with them. Other than you, those are the only people who will see it.

WHAT IT SHOULD TELL THEM

When others look at your plan — whether it's you, a parent, or a teacher — they should be able to figure out a few things pretty easily:

» What your business does

» How you do it (in other words, how you deliver your product or service)

» Who your customers are

» How you find new customers

» How much money you'll spend each month

» How much you'll sell your product or service for

» The resulting profit you expect to make

Anyone who reviews your plan should come away with a very good understanding of your business.

STARTING YOUR BUSINESS PLAN

Just as you did when you were brainstorming business ideas, it's good to have a quiet place to work without distractions while creating your business plan.

Up to this point, most of the work has been in your notebook. You'll want to make sure your business plan is completed on one or more blank sheets from your notebook. You should not have anything but the business plan sections on these pages. Better yet, consider creating your business plan on a computer. Your finished business plan is something you'll keep

and refer to often, so it should be created as a special document, not just a few notes.

To begin your business plan, use a clean page in your notebook or open a new document on your computer.

Your business plan doesn't have to be completed in one sitting and may take a few days — you may even want to do one section a day until it's finished. Creating a business plan isn't complicated, but you'll want to think about each section, so don't rush through it.

While completing this project, keep in mind that you'll be using your business plan while you launch your business. You'll also refer to it for the entire life of your business. Making a business plan is not just something you do because it's something you "should" do. It is very useful and will help you be successful in the long term. So, take your time and be as detailed as possible while creating your plan.

PLANNING YOUR PLAN

Business plans can have many different sections. The long business plans that large businesses create often contain many sections, but because your business plan is going to be for your own use, it can be a little simpler. The sections detailed in this project are the ones that will be most helpful to you as you start and run your business.

Your business plan will consist of four sections:

» *Overview:* This section gives a "snapshot" of your business, explaining exactly what your business does and how you deliver your product or service.

» *The Market:* Here, you include details about who your customers will be and where you'll find them. You also determine your costs and other money-related projections in this section.

» *Marketing:* In the Marketing section, you talk about the methods you plan to use to advertise your business.

» *Processes:* The last portion of your business plan details how you plan to run your business. The processes you outline in this section help you make sure that you get each step done.

OVERVIEW: WHAT, WHERE, AND WHEN

Your first business plan section — the Overview — describes your business. In two or three paragraphs, tell the story of what you plan to sell and how.

This section does not need a lot of detail, just the basics of what your business is all about.

WHAT YOUR BUSINESS WILL DO

Start by simply stating what your business is. For example, you might start with a sentence like this:

> *"Lucy's Cupcakes is a cupcake stand that specializes in selling the very best-tasting cupcakes to people in our neighborhood."*

Keep it simple and just say what you're going to do with your business. Beyond the first sentence, you should write a little more about your product or service and how you'll deliver to your customers. Remember, you don't have to go into a lot of detail right now. Just give a general description of what you'll do. For example:

> *"Lucy's Cupcakes sells homemade cupcakes to pedestrians and drivers, at a stand located at the corner of Maple and 4th Street."*

Notice that there is not a description of how the cupcakes are made or what the stand consists of (one table, two chairs, and a large sign, for instance). The overview section is not the place for these specifics.

PRODUCT VERSUS SERVICE

Your business will sell a product, a service, or both. *Products* are things. They are something that you can see and touch. Cupcakes, handmade bracelets, books, and video games are all examples of products that a business could sell.

A *service* is something your business does for people. For example, if your business provides dog walking, cleaning, lawn mowing, or car washing, you are providing a service. Your customers don't buy something from you that they can see and touch, so they are buying services.

Some businesses sell products and services. A great example of this is a car washing business that also sells air fresheners for the car. Washing cars is a service, and an air freshener is a product. Adding related products to a service business is a great way to increase income from your business.

Is your business going to sell products, services, or both? List your products and/or services here:

_____
_____
_____
_____

The Overview section is important and sometimes called the Executive Summary. Why is the Overview section such an important part of your business plan?

_____
_____
_____
_____

INVENTORY AND HOURS

One important difference between offering products or services is whether you'll need to carry an inventory. *Inventory* is a word used for the products you have ready to sell. If you are selling books, you may have boxes of books that you keep ready for when someone wants to purchase one.

The amount of inventory you keep depends on the type of products you are selling. For example, if you were selling bananas, you would not want too much inventory because the bananas could easily spoil before you sell them all. On the other hand, if you don't have enough inventory, you may not have products available when someone wants to purchase them. So, keeping the right level of inventory can be tricky and takes some practice.

In the beginning stages of your business, it's usually safe to have a limited inventory and then increase it as needed.

Much like product inventory, it's important to manage your time when offering services. You have only so many hours available to provide your services, so you don't want to sell more "hours" than you have available. If you are only able to walk dogs after school from 3:30 p.m. to 5:30 p.m. on weekdays, you have ten hours a week to sell. In this way, you can think of hours a lot like inventory. You won't want to sell 15 hours of dog walking and not be able to deliver, but you want to sell as close to 10 hours as possible — you don't want your hours to "go to waste."

How much inventory or how many hours will you need to have available to start your business?

_____

_____

_____

_____

WHERE YOU'LL SELL YOUR PRODUCTS OR SERVICES

While creating your business plan's Overview section, be sure to mention where you plan to sell your products or services. This is an important consideration. You want to make sure that you are meeting the needs of your customers while being aware of possible obstacles.

For example, the busiest street in your area may be the best place to set up a cupcake stand, but your parents might not let you set up there, or your city might have restrictions about selling in the area you pick.

Try to think of the advantages and disadvantages of different locations and sales methods before including them in your business plan.

GOING TO THEM OR STAYING PUT

There are generally two possibilities when it comes to where you will sell your products or services. Either you'll deliver what you're selling to your customers, or customers will come to you.

For many service businesses, it makes sense to go to the customer. Going to pick up your neighbor's dog for a walk probably makes more sense than making that neighbor bring the dog to you. After all, customers have probably hired you because they want to save time.

On the other hand, selling cupcakes door-to-door may not work as well. It's much easier to set up a stand and let customers come to you.

For some businesses, either model could work. If you start a car washing business, you could set up on a street corner and wash cars for people who see your sign while driving by. You could also go to people's houses to wash their cars for them. Either could be a great method of delivering your service.

CONSIDER YOUR LOCATION WITHIN YOUR MARKET

Where you live can be a big factor when deciding where to provide your products or services. If you live out in the country, where there's a mile or more between each house, going door-to-door could be a big challenge. It may be better to have customers come to you.

If you live in a city neighborhood, selling door-to-door may be perfect. However, also keep in mind whom you're selling to and what you think they would prefer.

Thinking about the business you have chosen, where do you think you should sell your products or services? Would it make sense to sell in more than one way?

_____

_____

_____

_____

HOW YOU'LL KNOW IT'S TIME TO START

The final part of your Overview section should indicate when your business will open. Consider what you learned about inventory levels and location. Will you need to do a lot of work before you can start doing business, or is your business something you can start right away?

If you plan to start a dog walking service, you probably won't need any sort of inventory to start, and you don't have to set up a location. You could start asking your neighbors if you can walk their dogs or start posting flyers in a day.

On the other hand, if you want to sell handmade bracelets, you'll want to create enough inventory to have plenty of bracelets before you start selling.

How many days will it be before you can officially start your business? Can you think of anything that might delay your start date?

_____

_____

_____

_____

MARKET: WHO, WHY, AND HOW

You also need to explain a few other details, such as whom you plan to sell to (who your customers are), why people will want to buy your products or services, and, more specifically, how you'll run your business.

While the Overview was an overall snapshot of your business, the Market and Marketing sections will each be more detailed. They can still be fairly short and to the point, but you'll want to list some specific details about your business here.

WHO WILL BUY FROM YOU

When you thought of your business idea, you probably pictured selling your products or services in your head. You might have imagined who your customers would be and what it would be like selling to them.

This is an important component of any business. Before you can begin to market your business or sell anything, you need to know who your customers are. Believe it or not, many businesses don't have a clear understanding of who their *target audience* (those who will buy from them) is. Not knowing enough about your target audience can lead to a lot of wasted time and money, so really take some time to think about this section of your business plan.

AGE, LOCATION, AND OTHER "DEMOGRAPHICS"

Start out with the basics. General information about your audience is divided into *demographics*. This is a term that's used to describe characteristics of a group of people.

Demographics can include age, occupation, where someone lives, whether someone is married or single, someone's gender, and how much money someone makes each year, to name a few. For the purpose of your business plan, you'll want to figure out a few factors:

» Age

» Location

» Interests, hobbies, and habits

AGE

How old do you think your average customer will be? You don't need to know an exact age, like 14 — just an age range. Will kids from 8 to 12 be most interested in what you're selling? Or will it be high school kids or adults?

What age range is most likely to want to use your business?

_____

_____

_____

_____

LOCATION

Knowing where your typical customer lives or spends time (known as *geographical information*) helps you decide where to advertise your business. It can also help determine where you set up shop. It may make sense to put up flyers at your local grocery store if you're planning a car wash in their parking lot, for example.

Where are you most likely to find your customers?

_____

_____

_____

_____

INTEREST, HOBBIES, AND HABITS

Once you know who your audience is and where to find them, it's important to know more about what they do. For example, if you start a car washing service, you know that your target audience will be people above the legal driving age, and you'll most likely find customers close to your home. But it's also important that they actually have a car and care about their car enough to have it washed. This has to do with their interests and habits.

What interests, hobbies, or habits are your best customers likely to have?

_____

_____

_____

_____

WHERE ARE THEY BUYING NOW?

Chances are good that whatever business you start, you'll be selling something that people can get from another business like yours, or you'll be providing a product or service that they currently have a different solution for. Any solution other than your business can be called *competition* or a *competitor*.

A competitor doesn't have to be another business. For example, if you start a dog walking service, your customers are probably either using another dog walking service already, or they are walking their dogs themselves. Either solution is competing with your business. If you're selling cupcakes, you know that people can buy cupcakes at the store, or they can make them at home. These other solutions are competition for your business.

*Just because there is another solution for customers'
needs doesn't mean your business isn't a great idea.
Very few businesses are started from an idea no one
has ever heard of before. As long as you have a way
to make your business seem like a better idea than
the customer's current solution, you can be
successful.*

In the Market section of your business plan, write about how
potential customers are currently getting the products or
services you plan to provide.

**Is there more than one solution for the problem you'll be
solving? List the possible other solutions people are now
using.**

_____

_____

_____

_____

WHY THEY WILL WANT TO BUY FROM YOU

After you look at where people can buy your products or
services, other than from you, you need to figure out why your
customers will want to switch from their current solution to
using your business.

Even businesses that have a lot of competition can be successful.
How many gas stations or grocery stores are in your town?
Chances are there are at least a few. But each one could be
successful by offering a reason for people to use its business
instead of another.

In the case of a gas station, it could have lower priced gas,
employ friendlier sales clerks, or be more conveniently located.
Any of these advantages could be enough for people to choose
one gas station over another.

YOUR UNIQUE ADVANTAGE

What advantages do you have over your competition? If you really think about it, you can probably come up with several.

Take a dog walking business as an example. Some potential advantages you could have over people walking their own dog are

» Hiring you to walk their dog can save them a lot of time.

» You might become a much-needed friend to their dog.

» You will pick up the dog droppings along your walk — something no one, including your customer, wants to deal with.

As an advantage over another dog walking service, you may have a better price. People in the neighborhood may find you more reliable, or maybe their dogs like you more than other dog walkers.

In many cases, you can create the advantages your business offers just by thinking about what might be wrong with the competition. Are they too expensive? Is their product flawed in some way?

You can make sure you have a unique advantage by setting your pricing right and making sure that you offer the best service and quality.

What are two to three advantages you have over your competition?

_____

_____

_____

_____

WHO ARE MY CUSTOMERS?

To determine more about the market you'll sell to, use this market survey with people who are in the area where you'd like to sell your product or service. Feel free to add questions that relate to your specific business.

Suggested script:

Hi, I'm considering starting a business that will (sell or do what?). Do you mind if I ask you a few questions to get an idea of who my target market is?

Questions:

Is what I described something you currently buy or would buy? Why or why not?

_____

_____

_____

_____

If you do currently buy what I described, where do you get it now?

_____

_____

_____

_____

What do you like most about buying from _____?

_____

_____

_____

_____

What's something you'd change about buying from _____?

_____

_____

_____

_____

If you don't mind me asking, what is your age range?

< 20

20-30

31-40

41-50

51-60

60+

Are you married or single? _____

When not at home or work, where do you spend most of your time?

_____

_____

_____

_____

What is your favorite hobby?

_____

_____

_____

_____

Note: Be sure to thank those who participate in your survey for helping you plan your business strategies.

MARKETING: COMMUNICATING YOUR ADVANTAGE

It isn't enough for you to know that you're a better choice than your competition. You have to make sure that your potential customers know it, too. You can have the best cupcakes in the world, but if you don't get the word out about them, you won't sell very many.

JUDY'S CUPCAKES

We have the freshest, best-tasting cupcakes in the world!

Try our secret family recipe, and you'll never want any other cupcake.

Find us at the
Corner of Maple & 4th Street
Saturdays from 12:00 p.m. to 4:00 p.m.

Getting the word out about your product or service is called *marketing*. You see marketing everywhere you look. There are commercials on TV and on the radio, billboards near roads, banner ads in games you play and websites you visit, and flyers pasted on telephone poles. Even some bumper stickers are a form of marketing.

Having a successful business involves a lot more than effective marketing — like providing high quality and friendly service — but marketing is a critical piece of business success. It's how people know your business exists, and it's how you communicate why they should use your business.

For the business you're building now, you won't be running TV or radio commercials or placing ads in magazines and newspapers. But you will definitely want to do some simple forms of marketing. Here are some ideas:

» Create a flyer stating what your business does, why you are the best, and how to reach you.

» Make several copies of your flyer.

» Post your flyers on bulletin boards at your local grocery store or laundry mat.

» Bring your flyers door to door (with your parents' permission).

What other ideas do you have for marketing your business to your target audience?

_____
_____
_____
_____
_____
_____
_____

PROCESSES: HOW YOU'LL DELIVER

The last section of your business plan is an important one. The Processes section explains how your business will do what it does. This section doesn't have to be several pages long, but it should have some good details about how you'll run your business.

Think about everything it will take to build and run your business and then explain it in this section. If your business is washing cars, for example, what materials will you need to get the job done? What steps will you take to complete a car washing job for a customer?

If people were to ask how your business works, they should be able to find the answer in the Processes section of your plan. Take some time to work through all the processes of your business, and detail them in this section of your business plan. Start with someone saying "yes" to buying what you sell. What happens after that? What should you have done before that point? List all the steps of your processes and be ready to add to the list as your business takes off.

RESOURCES NEEDED

Whether you are performing a service or selling a product, you will need certain resources to get the job done. If you're making a product, you will need the parts that make up your finished product, such as string and beads for bracelets.

If you're offering a service, you'll probably need some supplies to complete your jobs. For washing cars, you'll need a bucket, some soap, a sponge, and a towel for drying. For dog walking, you'll need bags to pick up waste, and it would be a good idea to have a couple of leashes in case a dog owner doesn't have one for you to use.

While you're listing the items you'll need for your business, also learn the costs of the items and include a list of one-time and ongoing expenses in this section of your business plan. You'll be able to update your ongoing expenses as you build your business and learn more about what your costs will be.

PROCESSES

It is important to think out the processes for your business. You need to know exactly how you are going to perform your service or deliver your products.

If you're making your products, you need to know the steps necessary to create them. If you're buying them, where will you get them? How much will you order, and how often? Once you have products to sell, how will you deliver them to your customers?

Walk through the entire process in your head and write down every step and material needed to create or do whatever you're selling.

To make sure that you don't miss anything, perform a test run of your product or service. Wash your mom's car after telling her what she'll get with her wash and answering her questions. Create a sample bracelet, writing down the steps as you go.

How many steps are there in your sales process? Can you remove any steps while keeping the quality of your product or service high?

_____

_____

_____

_____

YOU'VE COMPLETED YOUR BUSINESS PLAN. Congratulations! Planning is one of the most important parts of building a business. By learning to plan properly, you can experience success as an entrepreneur.

But what do you do with your business plan, now that it's finished? Formal business plans are often used to get investors or present a business idea to a bank for a business loan. Beyond that, business plans are also used by entrepreneurs to guide them after the business is started. That's why a good business plan is so important — it gives you a valuable tool to go back to throughout the life of your business.

IT'S ALIVE! (WELL, A "LIVING" DOCUMENT)

People often compare a business plan to a map. If you go on a long trip, it's hard to know where you're going without a map to guide you. In that way, we agree that business plans act like maps. However, maps don't change very much. Sure, new roads are built occasionally, and once in a great while the name of a town may even change. But for the most part, maps stay pretty much the same.

Business plans are *living* documents. In other words, they are not meant to be created once and then put in a drawer, never to be seen again. They are meant to change with the changing needs of your customers and your business.

As an example, think about companies that make computers. Have you seen old computers from the 1980s? They were big and bulky, they had one-color screens with no graphics (usually a black screen with green letters), and compared with today's computers, they were very slow.

What if a company making computers back then never updated its business plan? If the company was still making computers like it did 30 years ago, do you think it would sell any? No; in fact, it would have gone out of business a long time ago.

Even companies that don't sell high-tech products experience changes in the marketplace that make it necessary for them to change their business plan to keep their business healthy. Look at the milk industry. Not many years ago, if you went to the milk section of your local grocery store, you found cow's milk — skim milk, 1% milk, 2% milk, and whole milk. You would have also seen buttermilk, cream, and other milk-based products right alongside the milk, but it was all some sort of milk.

Which would you buy?

Today, most grocery stores' dairy sections have the same milk products, but they also sell soy milk, almond milk, coconut milk, and several other milk-like products that don't contain any cow's milk. And other milk products have been added as well, like lactose free milk and several varieties of flavored milk.

All this competition to plain old milk didn't exist when the milk companies first created their business plans, but now there is a ton of competition for them to be worried about. So, you can bet their plans have changed to account for the extra competition. For starters, most dairies run much *leaner* operations now, meaning that they have had to cut back on waste and improve their production methods to be more efficient. The milk industry also advertises a lot more than it used to.

Whatever type of business you build, you can be sure that things will change, and that's okay. Just be sure that your business plan stays up-to-date with the changing conditions around you.

In fact, your business plan should be reviewed and updated a few times a year to make sure that it still matches with your business goals and your target market.

PLAN FOR CHANGE

One thing you can be sure of is that changes will take place that will affect your business. Some changes are good, and some can be challenging, but the only thing that is for certain is that changes to your plan will be necessary at some point. Changes are how the world moves forward, so don't be afraid of change. Instead, expect change and be ready for it.

How can you be ready for change? Well, just knowing that things will change is a great first step. People who are always surprised when anything changes have a hard time getting used to change. They often resist it, and while resisting some changes can be a good thing, it's better to embrace many types of change.

Here are two examples of the types of changes that could affect your business.

EXAMPLE 1: TWO CHALLENGING CHANGES

Dillon started a cupcake business a couple of months ago. He created his business plan, which listed all his costs and how much he would sell a cupcake for, and he included information about where his cupcake stand would be located.

Things were going great, until the owner of the empty lot, where he set up every Saturday, told him that he needed to use the lot for something else, so Dillon couldn't sell his cupcakes there anymore. This Saturday would be the last day he could sell from that location.

In addition to that bit of bad news, the last time Dillon went to the store with his mom to buy ingredients for his cupcakes, the price of sugar had doubled from the time before. It seems the cane fields in Hawaii flooded earlier in the year, which created a shortage, driving up the price. With the higher cost of sugar, Dillon's profits were going to be slim going forward, unless he raised his prices.

What would you do about the first change that affected Dillon's business?

_____

_____

_____

_____

If you were in Dillon's place, how would you handle the increase in the cost of sugar?

_____

_____

_____

_____

EXAMPLE 2: A POSITIVE CHANGE

Maria created her business plan for selling homemade bracelets about a month ago. Business had been going well, even though she was not allowed to sell bracelets at school. The school's handbook stated that students were not allowed to sell things on school grounds, and Maria's business plan accounted for that restriction.

Then, last week, a new principal, Ms. Brown, started at Maria's school. Ms. Brown made it clear that she wanted to include more in the school's curriculum to encourage business and entrepreneurship. One change she made right away was to allow students to sell on the school campus, as long as it was before or after school or at lunchtime.

This change meant that the demand for Maria's bracelets was about to increase!

What changes will Maria need to make to her business plan to account for the new policy at her school?

_____

_____

_____

_____

PREPARING FOR CHANGE

To prepare for change in your business, take a look at each section of your business plan. What might change in the market, in your ability to sell, or in your goals that would make it necessary to change your plan in some way?

List two to three potential changes, along with some ideas about how you would adjust your business to accept the changes.

KEEP IT HANDY AND GIVE IT ATTENTION

Your business plan isn't something to be thrown in a drawer and forgotten. Because it's important to update it regularly, you'll want to make sure that you keep it easily available to you. Some entrepreneurs even pin their business plans to the wall next to where they work. This keeps their plan at the top of their mind and makes it easy to refer to as needed. (Of course, you'll want to get your parents' permission before pinning anything to your wall.)

Where will you keep your business plan?

_____

_____

_____

HOW ARE YOU DOING?

One of the best reasons for creating a business plan is that it helps you track how you're progressing in building your business. Your business plan lays out how you do what you do, and reviewing it as you build and run your business can keep you on track. This makes your business plan a valuable tool for tracking your progress.

Anytime you aren't sure what to do next, refer to your plan for guidance.

Go back and review your completed business plan. Should anything be added to your plan or changed? How often will you review your plan to make sure it's up-to-date?

_____

_____

_____

PROJECT 5 BUDGET FOR SUCCESS

THERE ARE MANY REASONS TO START A BUSINESS: IT CAN BE A LOT OF FUN; IT CAN GIVE YOU A SENSE OF PRIDE AND ACCOMPLISHMENT; YOUR BUSINESS CAN HELP PEOPLE; AND YOU COULD EVEN BECOME FAMOUS. But there is one thing that every business has in common, and that is that one of its goals is to make money.

In this project, you'll discover how to properly handle money. You don't have to be a whiz with numbers or an accountant to learn how to manage money in your business. You just need a basic understanding of how money flows through your business.

PROFIT, COST, AND SALES

Money may not be No. 1 on your list of reasons for starting your business, but it's bound to be somewhere on your list. After all, if your business doesn't make a *profit* (the difference between the money you take in and the money you spend), you won't have a business for long.

Money in business can generally be divided into two categories:

» Costs

» Sales

What are your top three reasons for wanting to start a business? Is making money near the top of your list?

_____

_____

_____

_____

COSTS

Costs are also called *expenses*. This is the money that flows out of your business. Every business has costs associated with it. Costs can include the money you pay for supplies, inventory, marketing, and salaries and benefits for employees (if you have them). Other possible costs include equipment and machinery, gas and maintenance for a car (if you or your parents use one for your business), shipping (if you send things to your customers), and various services you may pay for, such as a cellphone or Internet access.

Large companies have many more expenses that you won't have to worry about. They often have buildings, fleets of cars or trucks, lawyers and accountants, and large advertising budgets to pay for.

SALES

The money you collect from your customers can be called your sales, or *revenue*. This is the money that flows into your business, and it includes any money you collect from customers for the products or services you sell. If your business is healthy, this number is larger than the total costs of your business.

DECIDE HOW MUCH TO CHARGE

One of the first money-related tasks you have when starting a business is deciding how much to charge for your product or service. This can be a bit tricky. You want to charge enough to make a nice profit, but if you charge too much, no one will buy from you, so you won't make any money at all. Striking a balance somewhere in the middle is your goal.

A lot of factors can go into deciding how much to charge your customers, but two factors are most important:

» Competition

» Costs

COMPETITION

When figuring out what to charge customers, competition includes any option the customer could choose over the one provided by your business. This could be a product or service at another business like yours, or it could be the expenses they would pay to do it themselves.

For example, if you start a car washing business, your customers could go to a carwash and pay for that service, or they could do it themselves. Either way, expenses are involved: They have to pay the carwash, or they have to buy soap and sponges to clean their own car.

When looking at possible competition, don't forget to account for the customer's time.

If they wash their own car, that won't cost them very much money at all. They probably have soap in their home already, and they might have sponges and towels for the job as well. But most people don't have much extra time, and that is worth a lot to many people. If they hire you to wash their car, it saves them the time it would take to drive to a carwash or do it themselves.

Also consider convenience as a factor when looking at your competition.

Not only is washing their own car taking up a lot of your customers' time, it's also very inconvenient. They have to get out all the supplies, work hard to get their car clean, and probably get all wet in the process. Then they have to dry the car, put all the supplies away, and wash and dry any towels they used. What a pain!

Convenience and time are also factors if you're selling products rather than a service. Delivering products to your customers at their homes saves them a lot of time and is much more convenient than going to a store or even shopping online.

So, when figuring out what to charge for your product or service, look at what it costs your customers to use your competition and then decide how much the time savings and convenience of your business is worth. This may be hard to judge at first, but there's a simple solution: Ask people.

Go to the people who are your potential customers and ask them what they think is a fair price for your product or service. If you ask enough people, you'll get a range of answers that will give you a good idea about how much you can safely charge your customers.

Name two to three competitors your business will face. How much does each competitor cost your customer?

YOUR COSTS

The most important factor when deciding what to charge for your products or services is your costs. Fortunately, figuring your costs of doing business is pretty easy.

Figure out your costs in terms of how much you'll spend each month. You'll have two types of costs to consider:

» One-time expenses

» Ongoing expenses

One-time expenses are things like a bucket for your car washing business. You may need to replace your bucket at some point, but it isn't something you'd have to buy every month, so it would go in the one-time expense category.

Ongoing, or *recurring*, expenses are those that you have to pay every month (or even every week). For example, if you have a cupcake business, you'll need to buy flour again and again. It's not an expense you'll experience once and never have to buy again.

List all the expenses you can think of in your notebook and put them in two columns: one for one-time expenses and one for recurring expenses.

For recurring expenses, figure out your cost on a monthly basis. So, if you'll have to buy flour every two weeks, multiply it by two to cover your costs for a month.

For one-time expenses, divide them by the number of months you think it will take before you need to spend that money again. For example, if you think you'll need to buy a bucket for your car washing business twice a year, divide the cost of one bucket by six. If you think something will last more than a year or never need to be replaced at all, simply divide that cost by 12 to get your monthly cost.

Bucket for washing cars

Cost: $5.00

Will need to replace twice per year
(every 6 months)

$5.00 ÷ 6 months

5 ÷ 6 = $0.83 per month

What are the top three costs in your business?

_____

_____

_____

_____

DON'T FORGET YOUR TIME

Just as you considered your customers' time when comparing your business with your competition, consider your own time when looking at your costs. Your time is valuable, and you don't want to ignore the time it will take to provide your products or services to your customers.

If you're selling handmade bracelets, and the materials for each bracelet cost you $2, you need to charge more than $2 to make any profit. Simple, right? But are the costs of your materials and supplies your only costs?

Say your cost of materials is $2 each. If you decide to sell the bracelets for $3 each, that is a profit of $1 per bracelet. If you sold 100 bracelets, that's $100 in profit. Pretty good! But what if it takes you an hour to make each bracelet? Then you're paying yourself only $1 per hour for your time. Is your time worth more than $1 per hour? It definitely is!

How much time will it take you to provide one product or service to one customer?

_____

_____

_____

_____

Based on your costs and your competition, how much will you charge for one of your products or services?

_____

_____

_____

_____

FIGURE OUT YOUR PROFITS

After you know how much it will cost you to run your business and how much you'll charge your customers, you can easily figure out your profits. For now, focus on figuring out how much profit you'll make from selling one product or service to a customer. This will take a bit of guessing in the beginning, but that's okay. You'll be able to adjust your numbers as you build more experience with your business.

To figure out your profits:

1 **Guess how many products or services you'll sell in one month.**

Be sure to keep in mind the amount of time you have available and be realistic with this number. It's great to have a big goal, but if you set it too high, you may become discouraged if you don't reach it. Starting with a lower guess in the beginning is fine.

2 **Multiply your guess by the amount you'll sell a single product or service for.**

That amount is how much money you can expect to take in within one month.

3 **Now take the amount you'll make in a month and subtract your monthly expenses.**

The result is your expected profit for one month of business.

How much money do you expect to make each month?

Are you happy with the amount you have calculated as monthly profit? What is one thing you could do to increase your profit each month?

_____

_____

_____

_____

Calculating Profit

	Selling price of one product or service
x	Number sold in a month
=	Monthly revenue

	Monthly Revenue
-	Monthly Expenses
=	Monthly Profit

KEEP TRACK OF YOUR MONEY

One of the most common reasons that a business fails is mismanagement of money. In other words, they go out of business because they aren't making wise decisions about money. So, keeping track of all the money going in and out of your business is very important.

Basic tracking of the money in your business is called *bookkeeping,* and it's something you'll do daily (or at least any day that you sell or buy anything for your business). You'll also do a little extra work at the end of each month to total everything up and see how much profit you made.

HOW MUCH IN, HOW MUCH OUT?

Bookkeeping for most small businesses can be completed in a few minutes a day. You can keep your books in several ways. You can

» Use a notebook with lined paper

» Purchase a *ledger* (a book designed for entering all your company's income and expenses)

» Use a program on your computer

» Use the ledger page provided in this project

DAILY LEDGER FOR

_____

(BUSINESS NAME)

MONTH: _____

Date	Description	MONEY IN	MONEY OUT	BALANCE
		$	$	$
		$	$	$
		$	$	$
		$	$	$
		$	$	$
		$	$	$
		$	$	$
		$	$	$
		$	$	$
		$	$	$
		$	$	$
		$	$	$
		$	$	$
		$	$	$
		$	$	$
		$	$	$
		$	$	$
		$	$	$
		$	$	$
		$	$	$
		$	$	$
		$	$	$
		$	$	$
		$	$	$
		$	$	$
		$	$	$
		$	$	$
		$	$	$
		$	$	$
		$	$	$
	TOTALS:	$	$	$

Profit/Loss = (B)_____ - (A)_____ | $

Whatever you use to keep track of your money, be sure to accurately list every expense that you pay out and every amount you collect from customers. At the end of the month, you'll add up your *expenses* (money going out of your business) and *revenue* (money coming into your business), and you'll be able to see whether you've made a profit or lost money.

DAILY LEDGER FOR

Sample Business
(BUSINESS NAME)

MONTH: _September, 2017_

DATE	DESCRIPTION	MONEY IN	MONEY OUT	BALANCE
				$150.00 **(A)**
9/3/17	5 pounds of flour	$ -	$ 2.49	$ 147.51
9/4/17	1 dozen cupcakes sold	$ 18.00	$	$ 165.51
9/5/17	6 cupcakes sold	$ 10.00	$	$ 175.51
		$	$	$
		$	$	$
	TOTALS:	$ 28.00	$ 2.49	$175.51**(B)**
Profit/Loss = (B) _175.51_		- **(A)** _150.00_		$ 25.51

You're likely to have more one-time expenses your first month, so losing a little money the first month is to be expected.

Once your business has been going for a few months, you should start seeing some profit. If not, it's important to look at your expenses to see where you can reduce your spending. You can also review your pricing to make sure that you're charging enough for the products or services you're providing.

What will you use to keep track of your money? Will you remember to enter your expenses and income each day?

_____

_____

_____

_____

HOW TO MANAGE WHAT'S LEFT OVER

Hopefully, you'll start to make profits with your business pretty fast, and you'll begin having money to manage. This is a great feeling, and you should be proud of yourself for starting a profitable business.

Be careful. If you spend your money as soon as you get it, you won't end up with much to show for it.

Instead, set some goals, like this:

Goal	Amount	Reach Goal By
Buy a new bike	$140	August 1
Save money	$100	September 15

Notice that each goal is specific and measurable, and each has a deadline. If you set a goal like "I want to make lots of money" and don't specify how much money you want to make or by when, how will you know if or when you reach your goal? However, if your goal is to "make $200 by December 20," you'll know exactly when you reach or miss your goal.

Your parents may have advice or rules about what you do with your money, and one rule may be that you have to save some of it. We think that's a great idea! Learning to save money while you're a kid will help you through the rest of your life. If you save money, it will be there when you need it for a purchase, an unexpected expense, or even to start another business.

List three goals:

Goal	Amount	Reach Goal By
1	$	
2	$	
3	$	

REINVESTING

One thing you'll want to consider doing with some of your money is spending it on your business, or reinvesting. Reinvesting is important to any business. It's how you grow, and it helps to strengthen your business.

A reinvestment could help you market your business, offer more products and services, or improve in some other way. For example, if you have a cupcake business and are getting requests from customers who'd like to buy large cakes, you can expand your business by offering cakes. That may take a reinvestment of some of your profits for additional ingredients, cake pans, and boxes to deliver cakes in. Chances are good that it would be worth the reinvestment, but you won't be able to take that step if you don't save some of your money.

What are two or three things you could do to reinvest money back into your business, once you make some profits?

_____

_____

_____

_____

MARKETING IS A CRITICAL PART OF ANY BUSINESS. In fact, businesses that market well have a much better chance of survival than those that don't do a good job of marketing — even if their products or services are the same in every way.

This project teaches you the importance of marketing, covers several different types of marketing, and provides some ideas for how to market your business. We also dig into how to identify and define your target audience and how to best reach them.

PROMOTING YOUR BUSINESS

Marketing is the process of promoting your business. It's one of the most important things you can do to make your business successful. Think about it: If you had the very best quality product or service in the world, outstanding customer service, and the lowest price in town, your business would do really well, right? Well, only if people know about your business. If you're great in every other way but no one knows your business exists, you won't sell anything.

Marketing is what you use to get the word out about your business. When it's effective, marketing tells people what you do and why they should choose your business over another solution. It gets their attention and makes them want to use your business — or at least remember your business for when they need it.

There are many different types of marketing, from advertising (like you see on TV and hear on the radio) to the flyers you sometimes find on your front door at home. The kind of marketing that will work for your business depends on the people you're trying to reach, the budget you have for marketing, and the amount of time you have to market your business. The important thing is that you do some kind of effective marketing for your business. Without marketing, achieving success will be much more difficult.

List three marketing methods (other than the examples we list in this section) that you have seen recently.

_____

_____

_____

_____

GETTING STARTED WITH YOUR MARKETING PLAN

As with anything you do in business, you'll be more successful if you have a plan for your marketing. Figuring out the best way to market your business and then sticking to a plan to put your marketing methods into action will keep you focused and on the right track. Your plan will also help you figure out what's working and what's not.

Start your plan by finding a couple of blank pages in your notebook. Think of your marketing plan as part of your business plan. You don't want other notes on these pages — just your marketing plan. Just like the rest of your business plan, you'll refer to your marketing plan often, and you'll update it as needed.

Your marketing plan is another "living" document that will change as your business and the market shift. What works today may not be as effective tomorrow.

Why do you think it's better to start with a plan before beginning to market your business?

_____

_____

_____

_____

STEP 1: FIND YOUR MARKET

Your first task in creating a marketing plan is to figure out who your target market is, as well as where you'll find them. This step is important because marketing to the wrong people is a waste of time and money. It's far better to keep your marketing specific to the people who are most likely to purchase from you.

RESEARCH YOUR MARKET

Information about your market is called *demographics*. A full demographic profile of your market can tell you a lot about them. Some companies spend lots of money figuring out the demographics of their target market. They do surveys to determine their market's age, gender, income, *marital status* (whether they're married), number of children, and much more.

For your small business, it isn't necessary to conduct a lot of research and find out all these specifics. However, you'll want to be able to answer several questions about your target market, such as

» Where do they live?

» What do they like to do outside of work or school?

» How old are they?

» What problems do they have that your business might solve?

For many of these questions, you may know the answer immediately. For example, if you have a car washing business where you plan to walk to all your customers' homes to wash their car, you know that your target market

» Lives fairly close to your house.

» Owns a car and likes to keep it clean.

» Is old enough to drive.

» Would like for someone else to wash their car for them.

Knowing all this about your potential customers is important for marketing, because it helps you decide how and where to market to this group. For example, if you know your market is in a very small area of town, advertising on the TV or radio is probably not a good idea; those ads will go out to everyone in town, so much of your efforts are wasted. On the other hand, placing flyers on your neighbors' doors could work really well because you can be pretty sure you're reaching the right people.

Take some time to think about the demographics of your target market. Write a profile in your notebook to explain who your perfect customer is. It might look something like this:

> *The target market for Billy's Dog Walking Service is adults who live within five blocks of 234 Polk Street. They have at least one dog and are busy, so they have a need for someone to walk their dog for them. Also, their dogs are friendly and get along well with people and other dogs.*

This profile of an ideal customer for Billy's Dog Walking Service is short and simple, but it tells Billy a lot about how to market to his audience. He knows that whatever marketing he does should focus on a five-block area around his house; it should attract people who own friendly dogs; and it should appeal to busy people who are short on time.

What are the top three demographics that you need to know to market your business to the right audience?

_____

_____

_____

_____

SET REALISTIC BOUNDARIES

When considering whom you want to serve in your business, it may be tempting to think that your market is "everyone." If you're selling cupcakes, for example, you may recognize that just about everybody loves cupcakes, and you may be tempted to skip the work of digging deeper to define your target audience.

Whenever you're tempted to make this mistake, it's important to remember to be realistic.

If you truly wanted to sell cupcakes to everyone, you would have to consider a lot of factors. Some people are dieting and want sugar-free desserts. Some need food that's gluten-free. Others don't eat anything with eggs or dairy products in it. And, believe it or not, some people just don't like cake. If you try to appeal to everyone, you'll have tons of extra work ahead of you, and your business model could quickly become overwhelming.

To avoid this mistake, it's important to set boundaries when deciding on your target market. Be clear on what you will and will not provide through your business. If you get many requests for one thing you don't offer, it may make sense to add that to your offering later. But if you try to please everyone, it will be hard to please anyone.

This advice applies to the area where you plan to sell as well. It's easy to expand your offering to include people who live outside your original service area, but it's not so easy to reduce your service area once you've started. Start with a smaller area and grow as needed.

If any customers do ask for something you don't offer, and you aren't ready to offer it yet, simply let them know that you appreciate the suggestion. Tell your customers that while you don't offer that product/service right now, you'll let them know if you add it later. Then make a note of the request so that you can keep track of what your customers are asking for.

What is something a customer might ask for that you won't be able to do as your business is starting out?

_____

_____

_____

_____

STEP 2: REACH THE RIGHT AUDIENCE

After you have a good idea of who your customers are and where you can find them, you need to know the best ways to get their attention and get them to buy from you. Based on what your business does and whom you're selling to, you can make a good guess about what kind of marketing will be meaningful to your audience.

For example, if you're selling cupcakes, you know that people want certain things when buying a cupcake. First, they want it to look good and taste good. So, your marketing should include images of your cupcakes. The images should show how delicious your cupcakes look. Because taste is such an important factor in your business, part of your marketing may include handing out samples for people to try.

If you know that price is an important factor to your potential customers, you'll want to address that concern in your marketing. If you have the lowest price in town, be sure they know it.

If speed is something that's important in your business, share how fast your service is.

Make sure that, whatever you sell, potential customers are aware of why they should choose your business over any other.

What are two to three important points to mention in the marketing for your business?

_____

_____

_____

_____

STEP 3: CHOOSE THE RIGHT TYPE OF MARKETING

You can market your business in many ways. The type of marketing you choose should match what you know about your customers, be affordable for you, and do a great job of grabbing your audience's attention.

Some types of marketing you might consider for your business are

» Creating flyers to post at local stores

» Distributing cards or flyers door-to-door

» Holding a creative sign to attract passing traffic

» You or your parents posting about your business on Facebook

» Creating a YouTube video about your business

» Printing coupons to hand to people as they leave a store or other business

 Make sure to get permission from your parents before going online or walking around your neighborhood.

Of course, there are other types of marketing, too. Both large and small businesses use TV advertising, radio ads, print ads in magazines and newspapers, mailers that are sent to people's homes, and all sorts of online advertising. For your first business, it's best to start with something inexpensive and easy to put into practice. You'll learn a lot while putting your first marketing ideas into place, and you can always expand your marketing ideas later.

Of the marketing ideas we mention, which one will you try first? When will you start using this marketing method?

_____

_____

_____

GETTING CREATIVE

Make sure that any marketing you do is creative and unique. People see a lot of marketing every day, so you need to stand out from the crowd.

When creating anything that is printed, make it colorful and include images when possible. If your business involves cleaning anything, cutting lawns, or shoveling snow, take before and after pictures to use in your marketing.

Also, be creative in the ways you market. Try not to do what everyone else is doing. If you were taking orders door-to-door for cupcakes, do you think you'd get more orders if you brought along bite-sized samples for people to try? You bet you would!

List a marketing idea for your business that has not been mentioned in this project.

_____

_____

_____

_____

WORDS THAT SELL!

Looking for the right words to use in your marketing flyer? Here's a list of words often used in marketing that will help get the ideas flowing.

Adjectives that sell

Fresh	Pure	Strong	Trustworthy
Simple	Best	Honest	Smart
Easy	Handmade	New	Reliable
Friendly	Light	Spotless	Skillful
Bright	Dependable	Shiny	Riskfree
Delicious	Yummy	Tasty	Famous

Verbs that sell

Enjoy	Act (now)	Join	Create
Shop	Sign up	Enhance	Offer
Give	Save	Relieve	Provide
Restore	Earn	Give	Dream

Nouns that sell

Discount	Free sample	Confidence	Gift
Value	Family	Home	Leader
Time	Success	Member	Care

Write your favorites and your own ideas:

_____

_____

_____

Shipping Cupcakes to Customers in Another State

<u>Pros</u>	<u>Cons</u>
Will be able to stay in business	Will need to figure out how to ship the cupcakes
Can expand to even more states someday	Need to raise prices to cover shipping
Already have a customer list from home, so don't have to start over	Customers might be reluctant to have cupcakes shipped to them

IT'S JUST ABOUT TIME TO LAUNCH YOUR BUSINESS! But before you can declare you're open, you still have a few things to figure out. Your business plan outlines much of what you need to get your business off the ground. Now it's time to think even more deeply about what you'll need to run a successful business.

In this project, we break down all the steps you'll take to deliver your product or service and keep your customers coming back. By the time you finish this project, you'll be ready to open your business!

Before you begin work on this project, we encourage you to take a moment to consider how you feel about finally getting your business going. Record your thoughts in your notebook.

DELIVERING YOUR PRODUCT OR SERVICE

Having a great idea for a product or service is good, but it's only the first step to having a successful business. It's important to be clear on exactly how you'll go about getting your product or service to customers. People will expect you to deliver on what you say you'll do, so you must be prepared right from the start.

Think of it like this: Say that your mom and dad promise to take you to a cool new theme park that's in another state. They do a great job of describing what the park is like, and you're very excited to go. But on the day you're supposed to travel to this amazing park, you realize that your parents have no idea how to get there! Not only that, but no one has packed anything for the trip, the car is out of gas, and your mom forgot to ask for time off work. How disappointing!

The same disappointment awaits your customers if you don't have a detailed plan for delivering your product or service to them. You can have a great idea, market it well, and get people excited to make a purchase, but none of that matters if you don't deliver.

To make sure that you deliver in a way that satisfies your customers, you'll need to think about the three stages of your sales process:

» Before the sale

» Doing business with a customer

» After the sale

If you know what should happen during each of these steps, you'll be able to deliver in a way that keeps your customers coming back for more.

What are two dangers of not being prepared to deliver on your promises to your customers?

_____

_____

_____

_____

BEFORE THE SALE

A lot happens before your customers finally say "yes" to your product or service. They'll have to hear about your business somehow, such as through marketing you create. They may ask you questions about your product or service or about you or your company. And they'll weigh the advantages of buying from you or using other available solutions, like one of your competitors.

Everything you do up to the point where a customer buys from you is important. Your marketing should be great, you should have good answers to any questions that your customers have, and you should know why your product or service is the best choice for your customers. If you do a great job each step of the way, you'll increase the chance of people buying from you by quite a lot. On the other hand, if you aren't prepared for any one of those steps, you'll hurt your chances of success.

It's also important that you're prepared to provide your product or service as soon as possible after someone makes a purchase. You'll need to have your supplies or products ready to go before you sell anything.

You may be excited to get out there and make some sales, but if you aren't ready to deliver, it's a smart move to take the time to prepare first.

SALES IS PART OF THE JOB

Even though you may not think of yourself as a salesperson, you definitely are one. How do we know that? Well, everyone is a salesperson. Have you ever asked a parent whether you could stay up later than normal or whether you could have a toy or treat from the store? At school, have you ever asked a friend to trade lunch items with you? If you've done any of that, you've done what salespeople do.

When we examine what sales really is, it turns out that *sales* is simply the act of convincing someone to take an action. So, whether you're trying to talk your dad into buying you an ice cream cone or you're talking to a customer to get him to buy a product, you're engaging in a form of sales.

You'll sell throughout your life, so learning to do it well is a valuable skill. Even if you decide not to be an entrepreneur as an adult and don't work in a traditional sales role, you'll benefit from knowing how to sell when you want to ask your boss for a raise or get your own kids to go to bed on time!

 The key to almost everything in sales is knowledge.

Keep the following in mind:

» The more you know about your target market, the better.

» The more you know about what you're selling, the better.

» Knowing the advantages for the customer when he or she says "yes" is critical.

» Anticipating and knowing how to address objections is often the key to getting the sale.

In another project, we talk about why knowing your target market to properly market your product or service is important.

It's also important when it comes time to sell your offering to a customer. While useful, marketing alone is not enough to get people to buy from you. It lets them know that your business exists, and marketing can even begin to convince them to buy, but the final buying decision usually involves a sales process.

For example, if you're selling a car washing service, you might create a really nice flyer to post in your neighborhood. Say that Mrs. Finley from down the street sees your flyer and decides to call you. The flyer has informed her that your service is available, and it must have appealed to her enough to get her to find out more about your service. But until she speaks with you, no sale has been made.

When Mrs. Finley calls, she asks what kind of soap you'll use to wash her car. She wants to know how long it will take and whether you'll clean the inside of her car or just the outside. And even though she may not mention it, she is listening to make sure that you're someone she trusts to get the job done and take good care of her car.

If you don't have answers to Mrs. Finley's questions or if you aren't friendly, she may decide to use a different service. On the other hand, if you have great answers, sound friendly and helpful, and are able to explain why she should choose your service, chances are good that you'll make the sale.

In addition to simple questions about your product or service, a customer may also have *objections* (reasons a person gives for not buying a product or service). An example of an objection would be people saying they don't eat sugar when you tell them about your cupcake business. Having good responses to objections can turn people around so that they end up buying after all. For example, in response to the person who doesn't eat sugar, a great answer would be that you offer sugar-free cupcakes.

What are two objections you think your potential customers will have?

_____

_____

_____

_____

What are your responses to those objections?

_____

_____

_____

_____

THE MEANING OF CLOSING

One of the most important steps in the sales process is the closing, which is when a person finally agrees to purchase your product or service. The closing usually happens after you ask for the sale. Many sales people do a good job of answering questions and explaining their product or service, but make the mistake of failing to ask for the sale.

You may feel a little awkward about coming out and asking people to buy from you, but they expect you to ask. If you've done a good job answering people's questions, responding well to their objections, and explaining the benefits of your product or service, it should be natural to simply ask whether they'd like to purchase what you're offering.

How will you close the sale? Write the question or statement you'll use for closing.

_____

_____

_____

_____

DOING WHAT YOU DO

Someone has said yes to buying your product or service. That's awesome! Everything you've done to get your business ready — the planning, the marketing, and the sales — has led to this point. Now what do you do? It's time to deliver on your promises.

Not only is delivering on your promises the right thing to do, it's also good for business. For almost every business, having customers return and buy from them again and again is an important goal. Your local grocery store hopes you'll buy all your food from it, and your local salon wants you and your family to go there anytime they need a haircut. Even businesses that sell big items, like real estate companies and car dealers, want their customers to return to them when it's time for their next house or car, even though it may be years later.

The best way to get people to use your business repeatedly is to give them what you've promised them. You may be the best salesperson anywhere, but if your customers aren't happy with what you sold them, they aren't likely to come back. So, while you're delivering on today's sale, always take care to think about and plan for the next sale to the same customer.

How often do you think your customers will buy from you if you do a good job of delivering on your promises? (Daily, every week, monthly?)

_____

_____

_____

_____

What is one thing you can do to make sure that your customers want to come back and buy from you again?

_____

_____

_____

_____

DELIVER QUALITY

Have you ever purchased something or received an item as a gift that broke within a few days (or hours) of getting it? You probably have, and you were most likely disappointed in the product you got. You may have even felt angry or ripped off because the thing broke so easily.

Why did you feel that way? It's because you expected something other than what was delivered by the company that made it. You expected quality, and you didn't get it. And chances are good that you won't want to buy from that company again.

Keep this in mind when delivering a product or service to your customers. You want them to be happy with what they have purchased. In fact, you want them to be so happy that they'll want to come back for more — and maybe even encourage their friends to buy from you.

The way to get happy customers is to provide quality. If you're selling a product, it means the product does what it's supposed to do. If you're selling cupcakes, they should taste good and be fresh, not stale. If your product is handmade bracelets, they should look nice, and they shouldn't fall apart easily.

The same goes for a service. Providing quality in a service means doing the job that is expected. If you're washing cars, you get all the dirt off the cars, and you make sure the windows are streak-free.

In addition to the basics of providing what you promise, if you really want to wow your customers, take your quality to the next level by doing a little more than expected. Put a piece of candy on top of your cupcakes or use some wheel cleaner to get your customer's car wheels shining. There's no better way to get people coming back again and again.

What are three areas of quality your customers will expect in your product or service?

_____
_____
_____
_____

How will you make sure that you're delivering in each of the three areas you listed?

_____
_____
_____
_____

List two to three examples of extra touches you can add to your product or service that will really wow your customers.

_____
_____
_____
_____

TIME AND PROMISES

Time and the promises you make around the timing of your product or service are critical considerations. If you're offering a service, you'll need to keep a schedule of when you're available and adjust the schedule each time a new customer signs up. This way, you won't accidentally schedule two services at once. You'll also want to know exactly how long it takes you to perform a service from start to finish.

If you're selling a product, be careful about the promises you make about when people can expect delivery of their purchased goods or when more will be available. You may plan to sell your products only as you make them, but you may eventually get requests for more than what you have available. If you're making products, you need to know how long it takes you to make them, including the time to get the necessary supplies.

Before you start selling, experiment with your process and get the timing down. If you're washing cars, wash a couple of your family's cars and time yourself through the whole process. This way, you can be realistic about estimating how many cars you can wash in a day, and you can provide your customers with accurate times.

 If you're making something to sell, make several of your products, timing all the necessary steps as you go.

If you're making handmade bracelets, make five or six of them as a test. If you know it takes you 30 minutes to create each one and someone says she wants to buy 20 from you, you'll be able to give her a good idea of how long it will take for you to deliver her purchase to her. Twenty bracelets times 30 minutes would be 10 hours of work. Chances are, though, that you won't be able to work on your bracelets 10 hours straight, so you'll need to factor in all your other activities and obligations as well.

To keep your customers happy, it's important to do what you say you're going to do when you say you're going to do it. In the example of a car washing business, what if you schedule a car wash at 2 p.m. and don't show up at your customer's home until

2:45 p.m.? Your customer may not be home by the time you get there. Or, if she is home, she may be very disappointed that you didn't keep your promised appointment or may not have time for the car wash. Being late can damage your relationship with your customer, and it can lead to a bad reputation if word gets around that you don't keep your appointments.

Avoid the negative consequences of failing to deliver on time by knowing your business, your capabilities, and your schedule. Only provide time commitments you know for sure that you can keep and inform your customers as soon as possible if the product or service is going to be late.

How long does it take you to complete one product or service for your business? How many products or services can you provide in one week?

_____

_____

_____

_____

AFTER THE SALE

After you make a sale and deliver your product or service to your customer, you could just be done and move on to finding more customers. But you did a fair amount of work to get that paying customer, and he is still valuable to you.

It's a fact that it takes much more effort to gain a new customer than to sell again to an existing customer. This makes sense when you consider that your existing customers have already purchased from you. Their objections have been answered, and they're aware of what you and your company are like. They know what to expect from you.

Taking a few extra steps after the sale will keep your customers coming back without much extra marketing or sales effort. If you want customers for life, don't end your relationship with them after the sale.

APPRECIATE YOUR CUSTOMERS

Your customers have given you money for your product or service, and you could not be in business without them. Therefore, one of the first things you should do after a sale is show your customers that you appreciate their business. People like to feel appreciated, and showing appreciation can help you build your relationship with your customers.

Showing appreciation starts with a simple thank you at the time of the sale.

Saying thank you is expected when someone makes a purchase from you, so if you want to stand out from your competition, you can do many other things to show your thankfulness. A few ideas are

» Sending a handwritten thank you note in the mail

» Providing customers with a coupon to use on their next purchase

» Giving people a small gift after they make a purchase

You can show your appreciation in many ways, and what works best for you may depend on the type of business you have. If you have a car-washing service, giving customers a free air freshener for the inside of their car may be a good idea. For a product company, like a cupcake business, you could devise a loyalty program so that every tenth cupcake is free.

You can get creative with your thank you ideas, but make sure that you do something. Your customers will like it, and your business will thrive as a result.

How will you show your customers that you appreciate their business?

_____

_____

_____

_____

FOLLOW UP

If you want your customers to keep coming back, the best thing you can do is build a relationship with them. Thanking them for buying from you is a great first step, but what about after that? Once you send a thank you note or show your appreciation in some other way, don't let that be the last time they hear from you.

Staying in touch with customers is something every business should do. It promotes something called top of mind awareness, which means that people think of your business often — or at least when they need what you do. With all the marketing messages customers see every day, it's easy to forget about a business that doesn't stay in touch with them in some way.

You can use many methods to stay in touch with your customers. Here are a few examples:

» **Email:** If you ask all your customers and potential customers for their email addresses, you'll begin to build a list that can be very valuable to you as time goes on. You can use some free and easy-to-use tools to collect email addresses from your customers and send them messages from time to time. These email messages could be surveys to ask how they liked your product or service, coupons for a future purchase, or just a note to check in with them.

» **Mail:** For businesses that cater to customers at their homes, such as a car-washing service or dog-walking company, regular mail may be the best way to stay in touch. Just as with email, you can send coupons or simple marketing pieces that will keep your business at the top of your customers' minds.

> *Be aware that this option can be costly. You'll have to pay to have mailings printed, and you'll need to pay for postage.*

» **In person or by phone:** A simple and free way to stay in touch with your customers is to visit them or call them. This isn't the best option for every type of business, but for those where you go to their homes anyway, it can work very well.

> *Following up with your customers after they have made a purchase is a smart move, so don't forget this step. You'll be building a list of customers for a long time, and that list is a gold mine. It would be a shame to waste it.*

Of the methods described, which one(s) will you use to stay in contact with your customers? Can you think of other ways to stay in touch and keep your business top of mind?

_____

_____

_____

_____

ANTICIPATE UNPLANNED HICCUPS

One thing you can be sure of is that things will not always go the way you plan. Business is unpredictable at times, and a lot of factors can have unexpected effects on your business. The market may change so that whatever you're offering is no longer needed or wanted. You may run into problems with suppliers. Or a family change may force you to put your business on hold.

But while you can't see the future, you can definitely be prepared for most things if you expect changes and roadblocks. Anticipating these situations doesn't mean having an exact plan for every possible issue that could arise; it means having a method for dealing with issues, no matter what they are.

WHEN SOMETHING GOES WRONG

If you ask any entrepreneur on the planet whether he has had things go wrong in his business, every single one will say he has. But not all of them handle the struggles they face the same way. Some business owners see a problem as a challenge and a chance to learn. For others, problems get the best of them, and they can let them ruin their business.

In business, and in life, learning to deal with problems in a positive way is a valuable skill. None of us can eliminate problems from our lives, but we can all learn to face our problems in a way that will not let them get the best of us.

What is one unexpected problem that has occurred in your life?

_____

_____

_____

_____

How did you feel when this problem happened, and how did you deal with it?

_____

_____

_____

_____

BE OPTIMISTIC

When something happens that causes a problem in your business, keep in mind that it probably isn't as bad as it feels right now. In a few days or a week from now, the problem probably won't seem very big. In fact, chances are good that a year from now, you won't even remember the problem.

That means that there's a good reason to be optimistic about problems that pop up. Being optimistic just means that you know things will get better, and the problem (whatever it is) won't be the end of the world. It doesn't mean ignoring the problem or not taking steps to fix it.

Being optimistic helps in many ways. First, it makes you feel better. If you think every problem is the worst thing ever, you won't be very happy much of the time. If you can look at problems in an optimistic way, they won't ruin your day. Secondly, the people around you — your customers and people you work with — will admire your optimism, and it will make them feel more confident in your ability to solve problems.

For example, say that Jessica has started a cupcake business, and everything is going great. She is selling lots of cupcakes, and the future looks bright. Then, she finds out that her mom got a promotion at work, and it means moving to another state. Moving may mean losing all her current customers and having to start all over.

Jessica could look at this challenge as something really bad. She could decide that it's just not worth it and close her business for good. This decision is pretty sad, but if she isn't optimistic, it may seem like the only possibility.

On the other hand, if Jessica is optimistic and decides to find the opportunity hidden in this problem, she could turn it into something great. What if she decided to simply expand her business and make her cupcakes available through the mail? She would have to figure out the best way to ship cupcakes so that they survive the trip, but other companies are doing it, so she would know it could be done.

With a little optimism and creative thinking, Jessica could take a situation that seems like a big problem and turn it into a huge opportunity. And that's what you can do with most problems you face, if you're willing to be optimistic.

When a problem occurs in your life, how do you usually handle it? Are you optimistic?

_____

_____

_____

_____

After reading this section, how will you view problems now?

_____

_____

_____

_____

BE REALISTIC

Some people think that being optimistic means thinking positively no matter what and not necessarily taking any action. But it's important to be realistic at the same time you're being optimistic. Being realistic means looking at issues that arise in an optimistic way, but realizing that a solution needs to be devised. Just positive thinking alone won't do much for you.

If you have a garden and you see a lot of weeds in your garden, simply thinking "There are no weeds" over and over again won't make them go away. It's far better to see the weeds, know that it's a problem you can fix, and then pull them out.

If you know of an issue that your customers are having with your product or service and just say, "Oh, everything will be fine," and leave it at that, you wouldn't solve the problem. It's much better to look at the problem in a realistic way and come up with a creative, positive solution.

FIX PROBLEMS ON THE FLY

Anticipating problems ahead of time helps you be prepared to handle them *on the fly*. In other words, you should take care of your problems as they come up. As an entrepreneur, your time is limited, so having the ability to take care of things as they happen is an important skill. This often means being able to switch from one task to another without a lot of time in between.

As with any skill, handling issues as they come up is something that will improve with practice. If you feel as though you don't know what to do when an issue arises, take a little extra time to think it through and make a decision. As you practice this skill, you'll get better at it, and soon you'll be able to fix just about any problem on the fly.

DON'T WAIT

One thing you don't want to do when issues come up in your business is wait to handle them. You may not feel like facing a tough problem, but most problems get worse if not addressed. Very few ever go away on their own. So even if you aren't sure what to do about a problem that has come up, don't put it off. Start thinking of solutions as soon as possible. The sooner you begin to solve issues, the better off your business will be.

FIGURE IT OUT AND TAKE ACTION

Facing your problems in business is a big first step in solving them, but it takes a little more than that. It's important that you approach each problem with the intention to find a solution and take action.

Some problems can be solved by making a list of *pros* (advantages of a particular action) and *cons* (disadvantages of taking an action). Almost every decision has advantages and disadvantages, and making a list of each can help you decide which decisions to make.

For example, if you had a cupcake business that was doing really well and then found out that your family was moving, you might not be sure what to do. This is a great time to create a pros and cons list for the possibility of selling cupcakes long-distance.

Shipping Cupcakes to Customers in Another State

Pros	Cons
Will be able to stay in business	Will need to figure out how to ship the cupcakes
Can expand to even more states someday	Need to raise prices to cover shipping
Already have a customer list from home, so don't have to start over	Customers might be reluctant to have cupcakes shipped to them

After looking at the pros and cons of deciding to ship cupcakes out of state, Jessica will be able to figure out whether her decision is something she wants. In her case, it looks like all the cons are easily managed. She can figure out packaging; people are used to paying for shipping when ordering out of state. If she built a good relationship with her customers and has a great product, they will definitely be willing to order from her.

If you were Jessica, what would you decide to do? Why would you make that decision?

_____
_____
_____
_____

MAKE IT RIGHT

When a problem occurs that affects your customers, you have more to consider. Not taking care of customer issues the right way can hurt your business. If a customer feels like you don't care or isn't satisfied with how you handle an issue, that person may not be a customer for long.

Handling any problem as soon as possible is important, and this is especially true when it comes to customer issues. How quickly you can solve a problem for customers has a lot to do with how they react to the problem. If they aren't happy about a problem but you solve it right away, they'll probably be very forgiving. If you don't solve the problem, you could create another problem: an angry customer.

What is one customer issue you can imagine happening in your business? How will you handle this issue if it comes up?

_____
_____
_____
_____

REMEMBER YOUR CUSTOMERS' NEEDS

The better you take care of your customers, the better your business is likely to do. So, if a customer has a problem with something involving your business, it's important to consider his needs and what he's asking for. Most people are reasonable, and you'll often be able to do something simple to make them happy.

For example, if you have a car-washing business and your customer complains that you missed some spots, it's easy to apologize, go over the spots you missed, and promise to be more thorough next time. That would almost certainly be enough to satisfy your customer.

If a bigger problem happens, it may take more to make them happy. Say that you scratched a customer's car while washing it. You would apologize and promise it won't happen next time, but that may not be enough for the customer to be satisfied. You may have to give the customer the wash for free to make up for the scratch, or you may have to pay for the damage to the customer's car.

If you aren't sure how to make a customer situation right, ask the customer what he or she would like to happen. Most of the time, it won't take much to correct the situation. If you handle it really well, customers appreciate it so much that they may just be loyal customers for a long time.

After reading this section, how will you view problems now?

_____

_____

_____

_____

THINK OF WHAT'S BEST FOR THE BUSINESS

Although thinking of your customers' needs is very important, you also need to think about what's best for your business. If you start giving products or services away more than you need to, it can cost your business a lot. Not every complaint from a customer means that you have to give her something for free.

This is where asking customers what they'd like to happen comes in handy again. Most people won't ask for too much. You may be willing to give customers your product or service for free or at a discount, but they just want you to know about the issue and correct it next time.

Balancing what the customer wants with the needs of your business is another skill that you'll get better at over time. For now, it's best to focus on the customer's needs, but don't give away too much.

What is something that won't cost your business any money that you can do to make up for a mistake?

_____

_____

_____

_____

WHEN SERVING CUSTOMERS IS A TOP PRIORITY, YOUR CHANCES OF SUCCESS ARE MUCH HIGHER. In fact, businesses that do very well are usually those that take great care of their customers. This project covers the importance of great customer service and how to deliver it. We give you tips for handling difficult situations and for showing your customers how much you appreciate their business.

When you get good at delivering excellent service to your customers, you'll go far. If you fail to deliver great service, on the other hand, your business isn't likely to last long.

WITHOUT GREAT SERVICE, NOTHING ELSE MATTERS

Say that you have an amazing business idea for a product, you plan really well, and you launch your business. The quality of your product is better than anything else that competes with it, you're able to deliver quickly, and your marketing is working great, so everyone you want to know about your business knows about it. You also offer your product at a lower price than anyone else. Are you guaranteed to be successful?

This scenario looks very good. It seems like you have everything going for you, and you may think that success is pretty much guaranteed. But one thing could stand in your way, even if everything else is just right. That thing is service.

If you don't provide great service to your customers, almost nothing else matters. No one wants to buy from a company that treats them poorly. So, providing great service to your customers is one of the most important lessons any entrepreneur can learn.

Would you buy from a business that had a good product but bad customer service? Why or why not?

_____

_____

_____

_____

CUSTOMER SERVICE

Customer service is a term used to describe how you treat your customers. Any business can have good or bad customer service. It's how you respond to customer needs and how you communicate with customers — whether it's in person, by phone, through email, or by other means. Customer service is also how you handle customer complaints and concerns.

Great customer service can be a big factor in a company's success, and poor customer service can do serious damage to a company. If your customer service is outstanding, overcoming some of the obstacles you face may be easier. For example, if a customer is unhappy with something but you provide excellent service, he may overlook the issue or at least give you a fair chance to correct it. On the other hand, if your service isn't good, people will be far less forgiving about other issues.

Describe what you think is good customer service. What actions would you consider to be bad service?

_____

_____

_____

_____

CUSTOMER SERVICE IS IMPORTANT!

Customer service is crucial for your business for many reasons. While great customer service does tend to make customers more forgiving, it's more than just that.

First, good customer service often just comes down to doing the right thing. Treating people nicely and fixing the mistakes you make are just good things to do, and you want your company to be the kind of business that always does the right thing.

In addition to doing the right thing, good customer service is good for business. People want to come back and buy from businesses that provide good service.

More importantly, your customers will tell other people about their experiences with your business. If they've been treated well, that can be great for your business. It's like free advertising! However, if people tell others that they were treated poorly by your business, the others will stay away, and that can hurt your business a lot.

Have you experienced or heard any stories about bad service at a business? Ask your parents about a time when they

received bad service at a company. How did that make them feel about that business?

_____

_____

_____

_____

WHY WE LOVE CUSTOMERS

You literally could not be in business without customers. That sounds obvious, but some businesses act as though it isn't the case. Your customers are the reason your company exists. They are what keeps you going and growing. That's why we care about our customers and always treat them well.

You have good reason to be thankful for your customers, and when you are, it shows. People can tell when you really care versus when you're pretending to care. So, get comfortable with the idea that customers are your company's reason for being and be thankful for them.

What are two or three things you can do to show your customers you care about and appreciate them?

_____

_____

_____

_____

PUT YOURSELF IN THEIR SHOES

People who do the best at customer service are those who can put themselves in the place of their customers. Being able to imagine what it's like from your customer's point of view is important and especially helpful when a customer has a concern or complaint.

Say that you have a business walking dogs. You take Mr. Barker's dog, Barney, for a walk, and Barney gets off the leash and runs away. You try to catch him, but he's too fast, and you have to go back to Mr. Barker to tell him Barney has escaped.

You know that the reason Barney got away is that his collar was too loose, which wasn't your fault. So, how do you think you should approach this issue with Mr. Barker? Should you blame him because Barney's collar was loose? Should you say, "It's not my fault. You should have made sure his collar was tighter?"

In this circumstance, it helps to put yourself in Mr. Barker's shoes. How would you feel if someone just told you your dog had run away? You would probably be upset and worried about your dog.

If your dog walker started blaming you for your lost dog, that would just make you feel worse, and you'd probably not feel very good about the dog walker. In fact, you may get angry at that person, and you almost definitely would not want to use that individual as your dog walker again. You may even tell your neighbors about the incident, which could make them not want to use that dog walker either.

Now imagine if you thought about how Mr. Barker was going to feel and approached him with that in mind. If you went to him showing that you were very concerned for Barney, the conversation may be more productive, right? If you apologized for not noticing how loose his collar was, it would show Mr. Barker that you're taking responsibility for your part, and he may take responsibility for the collar being loose. After Barney is found, you'd probably still be Mr. Barker's dog walker, and you wouldn't get a bad reputation in the neighborhood.

That sounds like a much better end to the story, doesn't it?

In this example, what is one more thing you could do or say to keep Mr. Barker as a happy customer?

_____

_____

_____

_____

CUSTOMER SERVICE IS MORE THAN JUST BEING FRIENDLY

Good customer service includes being friendly to all your customers. A smile and a pleasant tone of voice can go a long way. But being friendly isn't all it takes to provide the best service to your customers.

Almost everything you do in your business is part of your customer's service experience. Providing a quality product or service is an important step, delivering on time and keeping your commitments is very important, and resolving problems quickly is also vital. All these things are part of providing a good customer service experience. So, be friendly, of course, but look at each part of your business as a factor in providing good service to your customers. Work to improve everything you do to create the best possible service experience.

It comes down to really caring about your customers. If you're friendly but unwilling to be helpful or show you care, it won't get you far.

PROVIDING WHAT YOUR CUSTOMERS WANT

Another great way to improve service to your customers is to provide the types of products and/or services they want. If many customers are requesting something, seriously consider adding it to your offering. Responding to requests shows that you care about your customers' wishes, and it's good for business.

This doesn't mean always providing anything a customer asks for. That could cost you a lot of money in the long run, and it would make it hard for you to focus on what you do best. It does mean considering what your customers are asking for and making a decision based on what's best for both them and your business.

LISTENING TO FEEDBACK

In addition to requests for certain products or services, listen to other types of feedback from customers. If you want to know how you're doing at providing your product or service and good customer service, no one is a better judge than your current customers.

If you hear that someone really likes something you're doing, consider doing more of that. And if you hear someone is unhappy about something involving your business, find out more and consider making some changes.

Feedback is so valuable that it's a good idea to ask for it, rather than waiting for people to tell you what feedback they have. To gather feedback, consider using customer satisfaction cards or surveys or simply ask your customers what ideas they have for improvements to your business. You'll get some valuable feedback that can make a very positive difference in your business.

How will you get regular feedback from your customers?

_____
_____
_____
_____

HANDLING CUSTOMER COMPLAINTS

As hard as you will try to please all your customers, chances are that you'll hear a complaint now and then. Complaints can be minor or very big. They can be about the quality of your product or service, timing, a mistake that was made, or how the customer feels he or she was treated by you or someone working with you.

It's very unlikely that you'll be able to anticipate every possible complaint, so rather than having a solution for each one ahead of time, it makes sense to know how to handle complaints in general.

You can apply certain rules to any complaint that comes your way. In each case, the important thing to remember is that the customer believes there is an issue that you need to resolve. Whether you think those customers are right, their perception (how they see things) is that a problem exists, and that's what you want to keep in mind.

Handling complaints from your customers isn't about proving you are right and they are wrong. If being right is your goal, you could win the argument, but lose the customer! It's better to look at the situation from customers' point of view and try to understand why they're not happy with the situation.

This doesn't mean you have to take the blame for something you didn't do. It's okay to explain the facts politely, even if it means pointing out that the customer is wrong in some way. Just remember that the customer is why you're in business, so you should always be polite and professional.

How do you think you'll feel when a customer has a complaint about your product, service, or company? Can a complaint be a positive thing? Why or why not?

_____

_____

_____

_____

CALM, COOL, AND COLLECTED

Whenever a customer comes to you with a complaint, the first step is to stay calm. Hopefully, you'll never have a really angry customer, but it could happen. If it does happen, it will be important for you to stay as calm as possible and let the customer say what he or she has to say.

One of the worst things business owners can do is interrupt their customer while the customer is voicing a complaint. It's important to let those customers finish what they have to say, listen to their concern, and try to understand their point of view.

Once customers finish stating their complaint or concern, then it's okay to respond and work on making things right. After they're finished is also a great time to ask some questions if you aren't 100 percent sure of all the details. Asking questions shows that you care and are interested in finding a solution.

For example, here's a customer complaint that could come up:

Tanner started his car-washing business a few weeks ago, and things have been going great. He has created some flyers with a list of his services and posted them near his neighborhood's mailboxes. Calls from the flyer have resulted in several appointments. Tanner has washed four cars and made a profit of $43 so far, which is a good start on his goal of saving for a new game console.

He has also learned a lot in the past few weeks, like the time Mrs. Reynolds complained after he washed her car. Tanner had thought he did a great job, and he was sure Mrs. Reynolds would be happy seeing the work he had done on her car. He asked her, "How does it look, Mrs. Reynolds?"

"It looks good, but I'm not paying you the full price," she said.

"You're not?" asked Tanner, feeling a bit confused.

"No, because you didn't apply tire-shine to my tires." Mrs. Reynolds didn't seem angry, but she was obviously disappointed.

Tanner paused and thought about what he would say next. The flyer he had printed stated that tire-shine was extra, and Mrs. Reynolds hadn't ordered it when she requested her car wash. His first thought was that this was not his fault. She didn't pay for tire-shine, so why should she expect it?

He knew he was right in this situation, but he also knew that he needed to make a good impression with every customer. It was clear that Mrs. Reynolds had misunderstood something on the flyer, so Tanner replied, "I'm sorry you expected the tire-shine to be applied. It's listed on the flyer as an extra $2 charge, but it may not be as clear as it could be. I'll look at redesigning the flyers before printing more. For now, how about I apply the tire-shine free of charge this time?"

Mrs. Reynolds was very impressed with the way Tanner handled her complaint. He obviously cared about his customers, and his reply was professional and friendly. This was better than with many adults she did business with every day.

"You know what?" Mrs. Reynolds said. "I see it on the flyer now. It's my fault I missed it. Go ahead and shine the tires, and I'll include a nice tip to cover that and a little more."

How well do you think Tanner handled the complaint from Mrs. Reynolds? Is there anything you would have done differently? If so, explain.

_____

_____

_____

_____

TURN A COMPLAINT INTO A WIN

A complaint doesn't have to be a bad thing. Complaints and concerns raised by customers can help you learn and improve your business. If you listen to your customers and are open to their feedback, it will demonstrate good customer service, but it can also turn those situations from a negative to a positive.

In fact, a customer can go from being very upset to being a loyal promoter of your business. If she has a complaint and you handle it very well, the customer will appreciate it. If she feels like you listened and really cared about the concern, you'll have done something many big businesses fail to do every day. This can create loyalty in your customers, and it can even turn them from someone who's unhappy with your business to someone who tells people how great your business is! This situation is what we mean by turning a complaint into a "win."

WORDS OF ENCOURAGEMENT

YOU ARE AWESOME! How do we know that? Because you either have read, are reading, or are considering reading this book. That puts you in a select group of kids who are preparing to grow up and do great things. It means that you're thinking about topics that many kids your age never consider.

Whether you're interested in learning about entrepreneurship so that you can go out and build big companies or you want to find out about the many other benefits that learning about entrepreneurship can bring in every area of your life, we're proud of you for taking this step. Great entrepreneurs have created companies like Facebook, Google, Amazon, and Apple, to name just a few. These companies have changed the way people around the globe live their lives.

Of course, most entrepreneurs don't start companies that end up as big as the ones we mention, and that's okay too. The projects in this book can help you navigate life as a doctor, engineer, teacher, or anything else you'd like to be. People who learn entrepreneurship are innovators. The world is changing rapidly, and those skilled in the lessons of entrepreneurship are leading the way, bringing amazing new advancements to the market.

So, yes, you are awesome!

You have started on a path that will lead you on quite a journey if you decide to follow it. Starting a business isn't always easy, and it can be downright difficult at times. You will encounter challenges. Some you'll see coming and know how to deal with; others will come out of the blue, and you'll need to figure out what to do. At some point, you'll probably deal with negative people who won't believe in what you're doing. They may tell you that your ideas are dumb and that they won't work, or they may even discourage you from being an entrepreneur at all. We're here to tell you that you can do anything you put your mind to.

Not every idea is a good one. While listening to sound advice, be selective about whom you take advice from. If someone has done what you want to do, the advice comes from experience and may be very valuable. If someone has no experience doing what you want to do, be careful about following his guidance.

Even with all the challenges that come along with entrepreneurship, it can be very rewarding, lucrative, and fun. You'll meet some great people, and you'll make the world a better place. And if your business is a success, the sense of accomplishment you'll feel is unbeatable.

So, stay on course and focus on making the most of anything you do. Don't give up too easily and don't let failures discourage you too much. We have all failed at something, and we will fail again.

The key to success is to keep going and keep trying after you fail. You may not remember, but you have some experience with this already. When you were learning to walk, you fell down a lot. If you had given up, even after falling down 20 times, you would never have learned to walk. But you didn't give up. You kept going and trying until you figured it out. Do the same thing as an entrepreneur, and your success is almost guaranteed.

We're excited that you're taking the first step toward entrepreneurship, and we'd love to hear your story of creating and running your own business. Send it to us, and we just might use it in our next book!

Email us at Stories@BizWarriors.com.

To your success,

Adam & Matthew Toren

GLOSSARY

THIS GLOSSARY CONTAINS TERMS FROM THROUGHOUT THE BOOK. Please keep in mind that in many cases, a word or term has multiple accurate definitions. The definitions here are the terms as we use them in the context of this book.

Bookkeeping: Basic tracking of the revenue and expenses in a business.

Brainstorming: A way to come up with ideas and solve problems.

Brick-and-mortar: A business that is located in a physical building versus online only.

Business plan: An outline of a business that explains what the business is about and how it operates.

Competition: Any solution that a potential customer may choose insteadof a particular business.

Demographics: Characteristics of a group of people, such as age, gender, income level, and so on.

Entrepreneur: A person who owns his or her own business.

Entrepreneurship: The act of being an entrepreneur; what entrepreneurs do (see *Entrepreneur*).

Expenses: Also called *costs;* the money that flows out of a business.

Inventory: Products a business has on-hand, ready to sell.

Layoff: When a company tells a worker his or her services are no longer needed.

Ledger: A book designed for entering a company's income and expenses.

Listening to your gut: Following a feeling inside (positive or negative) when thinking about an idea.

Marketing: The process of promoting a business.

Objections: Reasons a person gives for not buying a product or service.

Product: A physical item being sold that you can see and touch.

Profit: The difference between the money a business receives (see *Revenue)* and the money the business spends in the same time period (see *Expenses)*.

Pros and cons: Advantages *(pros)* and disadvantages *(cons)* of taking an action.

Recurring expenses: Those expenses that are paid on a regular basis, usually monthly.

Revenue: Also called *sales*, the money that flows into a business.

Rewards: A positive outcome.

Risk: Something that can go wrong.

Sales: The act of convincing someone to take a particular action.

Security: As related to work, knowing what the future holds for income and profession.

Serial entrepreneur: A person who starts one business after another several times.

Service: Something a business does for people.

Stability: The likelihood that a person will be in the same job tomorrow as today.

Target audience: Those people who are likely to buy from a business.

ABOUT THE AUTHORS

Brothers Matthew and Adam Toren are award-winning authors, serial entrepreneurs, mentors, and investors. They founded YoungEntrepreneur.com, which grew to be the largest social networking forum for entrepreneurs in the world. Adam and Matthew are coauthors of the book *Small Business, Big Vision: Lessons on How to Dominate Your Market from Self-Made Entrepreneurs Who Did it Right* (Wiley,) and the award-winning book *Kidpreneurs* (BPMG, 2009).

Equal partners in each of their business ventures, the brothers got their start in entrepreneurship at a very early age. When they were in elementary school, their grandfather, Joe, helped them set up a business selling little trick stunt airplanes at a local festival. They learned how to "wow" the crowd with some cool tricks and an amazing customer experience, and they sold out quickly. From there, they were hooked!

Matthew and Adam had one sort of business or another from then until today and almost always had several going at once. While in high school, they imported wholesale car stereo systems, made a catalog, and sold to their high school classmates. They also imported kids' magic kits from Hong Kong and set up shop in several mall kiosks, selling out before the holiday season was over.

Shortly after graduating from high school, the Torens used all the money they had saved up to purchase a struggling local pool hall. They mapped out a blueprint for success and expanded it into a jazz bar and café. It eventually became a favorite date night spot in their home city of Vancouver, BC, and the bar hosted a lot of private parties for the movie industry and other corporate events. They worked hard there, even sleeping on the couches at the business many nights, and they turned it around and sold it for a very nice profit in their twelfth month of business.

Today, Adam and Matthew are actively focused on their consulting business at BizWarriors.com, as well as several other niche businesses. They are advisors to many startup companies and invest in startups that have great growth potential.

DEDICATION

To our late Grampa Joe, who helped get us started on this amazing entrepreneurial journey.

AUTHORS' ACKNOWLEDGMENTS

We wish to acknowledge all those who have contributed to our success as entrepreneurs and writers. Thank you to our mother, grandmother, and grandfather for supporting and encouraging us in everything we've done over the years. Thanks to our wives and children for all the love and inspiration.

Thanks to Kelly, our Wiley editor, for consistently providing awesome suggestions and guidance. And thank you to our publisher, Wiley, for years of support.

Lastly, we would like to acknowledge all the amazing entrepreneurs whom we have been privileged to work with over the years. Whether as business partners, mentors, mentees, or colleagues, you have helped shape our entrepreneurial vision, and we're grateful to know you.

PUBLISHER'S ACKNOWLEDGMENTS

Senior Acquisitions Editor:
Amy Fandrei

Project Editor: Kelly Ewing

Copy Editor: Kelly Ewing

Editorial Assistant: Serena Novosel

Sr. Editorial Assistant: Cherie Case

Reviewer: Mia Ewing

Production Editor:
Tamilmani Varadharaj